How To Start Your Own Food Co-op

How To Start Your Own Food Co-op

(with a little help from your friends)

GLORIA STERN

Walker and Company, New York

ACKNOWLEDGEMENTS

I would like to thank Sue Ehlenberger for research assistance, and for her unfailing attention to detail.

Most of all, I would like to express my appreciation to all the kind and helpful people in all the co-ops and other organizations around the country who so generously shared their knowledge and their experience for the good of the cooperative movement.

Two organizations which provided invaluable assistance were the Cooperative League of the U.S.A., and the Food Co-op Directory. My special thanks go to Don Lubin of the Free Venice Co-op, for his help and advice.

First published in the United States of America in 1974 by the Walker Publishing Company, Inc.

Published simultaneously in Canada by Fitzhenry & Whiteside, Limited, Toronto.

ISBN: 0-8027-0431-X

Library of Congress Catalog Card Number: 73-83300

Printed in the United States of America.

10 9 8 7 6 5 4 3 2

For Eric, who
like the people in the cooperative movement,
is working for a better world.

Contents

chapter 1

Cooperative Buying: What Is It?

What do you do when the price of everything from steak to the lowly onion has almost doubled? What do you do when even the economy cuts of meat are out of range for the average shopper and the vegetables that you have bought after a long wait on line turn out to be wilted or spoiled? What you do is to take a new look at our marketing habits.

The supermarket, with its abundance of food and beautiful displays of fruit and vegetables, used to be a pleasant place to wander and make up weekly menus as the shopper found new and intriguing items on the shelves. Many markets had bright lighting and music that put most of us into a trance as we overbought.

But for more than a year now the store operators have noticed that customers wander instead from store to store to get the best buys, use coupons more frequently, and shop more carefully, examining each item for comparative costs, frequently turning to house brands.

The inflationary spiral that affected clothing, housing, and education has hit everyone—where they eat. It is a nationwide crisis, and an ongoing one with no real end in sight.

Even those addicted to eating daily have come up with resistance in the face of a recent 19.5% annual rise in food prices (see page 5).

Lawyers, mechanics, artists, secretaries, teachers, and students are all looking for alternative ways of buying good food at reasonable prices. New methods which have been quietly explored over the years are now going to have a chance to come into their own. Cooperation has become a course of action for people who never visualized themselves as part of any movement.

The first record of a good consumer cooperative goes as far back as 1844 with the formation of a cooperative in Rochdale, England, by twenty-eight weavers who later formed a cooperative mill. These people looked out on a world forever changed by the industrial revolution. They found that they needed a new economic philosophy to handle the gradual death of handcrafting and the one-to-one distribution system, one that would enable them to cope with their newly enforced status as a poverty class.

There have been no consumer co-ops that have managed to survive without some underlying philosophy to pull them through problems. It may be the very simple idea that is occurring to many people now: that in order to mitigate the endless need for higher wages to cover higher prices, they have to handle some of the rising distribution cost themselves, either through their own cooperative labor or management.

There have been many forms of cooperative ventures, both consumer- and producer-oriented, that have developed throughout the world since the early nineteenth century. The range of involvement is up to 40% or more among people where the concept has caught the imagination. The majority of the services in Finland and Iceland are owned cooperatively.

It was not until 1916 that the nucleus of the Cooperative League of the U.S.A. was formed in New York. The supermarkets with the "Twin Pine" symbol are among the many different producer, consumer, and service members of the League. It is estimated that there are about 24 million family members at this time, in affiliated member organizations.

The early twentieth-century credit unions, with their broad urban membership, were able to help finance housing cooperatives. They went on, through their individual members, to finance some of the giants of cooperative supermarkets in the 1930's, the Washington, D.C., Greenbelt chain and also one in the California Bay area. They are well past their growing pains and have proved for several generations that—with good management—food costs can be kept down while quality is maintained.

Again, in the Depression of the mid-thirties, there was a new impetus to watch every penny spent. In the best tradition of Americans in crisis, neighbors banded together to help themselves as well as others and formed food-buying cooperatives. The few surviving co-ops, started by earlier immigrant groups with their ethical traditions and experience, were able to aid the new stores.

Prosperity during World War II followed by financial optimism and an easier life almost stopped the consumer movement cold in the U.S. Many small stores and co-ops failed, as supermarket chains gave strong competition through greater selections of merchandise and cheaper prices. The surviving co-ops grew in size and frequently developed into marketing centers, but their members did not increase substantially. It was not until the 1960's that a new style of consumerism injected life into cooperatives.

The smallest food-buying co-op unit is a group of 6 to 12 families that simply go to the local wholesale market for produce, dairy products, and bacon, or health foods. It seems that things are still cheaper by the dozen, and whether the group purchases are just a selective food supplement to the usual supermarket or a total commitment, the savings and quality are there to be had. Other satisfactions are also to be had. Some middle-class executives and teachers even seem to enjoy the 6 A.M. excursion (as long as it is not more than once a month) to the big wholesale marketplace.

Modern supermarket-bred people are thrilled with the exciting atmosphere of a wholesale produce market, with acres of displays of fragrant strawberries, crisp green lettuce, baskets of perfect white mushrooms, mounds of shining purple eggplant, and sun-ripened fruit, with nothing rotting for days in plastic wrappings. There is something satisfying about buying in that abundant atmosphere and bringing back bushels of food at savings of up to 50% or more.

Despite the high price of wholesale meat, some co-ops devoted to meat-buying insist that savings are still possible. Others, like Julie and Bill K. of Los Angeles, buy their own family meat in bulk quantities from a semi-wholesale supplier.

Other, somewhat larger food-buying organizations, with 100 to 500 members or more, have been set up as a form of political or social action or as an alternative lifestyle. Many are run by dedicated teachers, students, business people, or dropouts who work part-time at minimum wages, as a form of community service. No matter what the lifestyle or political orientation is, there seems to be room for all, and the members of some are so varied that they appear to be a cross-section of the country. The success of these groups depends entirely on dedicated and competent management. Some almost floundered until they could learn to run what was, in reality, a small business grossing $250,000 a year. They may have their own beef grown naturally, without hormones, and stock health foods. Many have a depot or a store and supply as many as fifty smaller units of a few families each.

A growing number of new cooperative wholesale warehouse-stores are forming throughout the U.S. to supply the smaller groups and storefronts with lower cost supplies. Their individual membership ranges up to 4500 families.

A new and highly successful type of cooperative has been springing up across Canada for the past ten years. It is called a "Direct Charge Co-op" and its principles are now being explored in the U.S. as well. It may solve many of the problems that the cooperative movement is experiencing in the U.S. at this time.

The older cooperative supermarkets with shareholders have begun to expand into chains in both black and white working-class communities. They have the advantages of regular store hours and a larger selection of merchandise. A staff has the management responsibilities and the savings are still substantial but considerably less than the "do it yourself" co-op.

There are many reasons for forming a food co-op: the psychological pleasure of being a good provider, beating the system, a focus for a social or consumer action, avoiding impersonal and indifferent supermarkets, as a source of natural foods, or most important, the measurable savings on the weekly market basket.

If you do not have the temperament for fasting, perhaps it is time to start to join a food co-op. There is one that is right for you. What this book will attempt to do is to describe the different types of food-buying cooperatives, how they work, how they are formed, how to join an existing group, where and how to buy, and finally, to enable you to choose the kind of group that suits you individually.

PERCENTAGE CHANGE
FROM AUGUST 1972 TO JULY 1973

Consumer Price Index 1967= 100
Consumer Price Index August 1973= 135.1

FOOD	+19.5
HOUSING	+4.1
TRANSPORTATION	+3.3
HEALTH, RECREATION	+3.2
ALL ITEMS	+7.5

Source: Bureau of Labor Statistics

chapter 2

The Small Buying Club

Some neighbors have found that they can pool a little money and labor, eliminate a few middlemen and plastic wrappings to eat better and spend less. This may be the easiest and most neighborly of all the cooperative buying ventures. They generally buy just produce, perhaps cheese and bacon as well. (The most daring are meat-buying groups.)

Wednesday and Thursday mornings between 5 and 8 A.M. the freshest-looking produce in the most abundant quantities you have ever seen are for sale at your local city produce terminal. The terminal varies from Water Street in Chicago, the new Hunts Point and Bronx terminal in New York, to the Los Angeles Grand Central Market, but unless you have good local farmers, or a green thumb and a garden, you cannot buy better foods for less money. If you do not mind a few hours of work every four to six weeks, the savings are up to 50% for high-quality food. Each group surveyed has their own method of operation worked out to suit their needs and location. The simplest method is to charge a flat fee each week and divide the food equally.

What they do have in common is a resentment toward paying high prices for shriveled or spoiled produce. One co-op member said, "Not only are the fruits and vegetables beautiful, but we have never eaten so well. We have even tried new vegetables that we never thought of eating before, and now we have a salad and less starch for dinner." Others find it easier to have some of their shopping done for them and are pleased to discover what is in the weekly shopping bag. To insure that the surprise is not unpleasant, many groups keep a list of "never-nevers" and preferred foods. (Some people just won't eat kohlrabi.)

There is even a "mushroom and asparagus" co-op formed by the tenants of the Dakota, an elegant cooperative building in New York. They are looking for a cheaper source of higher-priced and out-of-season produce.

Since many of the crates contain multiples of twelve, it is easier to keep the group to six or twelve members. Groups have managed with varying memberships, but it becomes a little awkward dividing a case of twenty-four heads of lettuce. Unless you have a few station wagons available to use in rotation, stick to a small group. All the produce for a group of six or eight should fit in the average car.

It is also difficult to manage a cooperative that shops for more than twelve members unless you have a highly organized group willing to share responsibility, a large enough place to divide the food, and perhaps a pickup truck or two station wagons. The food can be divided in a church basement, community room, loft, porch, or even a large room in a member's home. With more people the savings on the weekly food budget increase, but so do the problems. There have been many examples of large groups working well, but only when members are compatible in both food preference and personal outlook. A group of any size can be pulled apart when some members want strict economy as the basic motive of the group, others are seeking either a chance to have luxury foods at savings or higher-priced natural foods, while still others are seeking a method of social involvement.

The most successful of the food-buying clubs are those whose members have similar sized families, food tastes, and a sense of responsibility to the group. If many families are away for the summer, it may be wiser to decide in advance to disband during these months. If a member family is going to be away for a few weeks, some attempt should be made to find a temporary replacement.

In a suburb of Boston, there are two clubs that are planning a reshuffle so that large families would belong to the same club. They are also thinking of expanding and adding dairy products. Since these clubs have eighteen members each, many of whom own station wagons, each week two members drive their own cars and shop together. This enables them to have a larger variety of produce.

Apartment buildings or off-campus housing facilities lend themselves easily to the formation of cooperative groups. One thriving New York City club of thirty families found that it is easy to shop in bulk for the last four years, since they all live in the same building. They take a few shortcuts, which reduces some of the savings but simplifies the amount of work involved. They preorder from one produce distributor in the wholesale market at Hunts Point, and a cheese wholesaler in downtown Manhattan. (They order $150 worth of cheese every three weeks.)

One woman has been in charge of the organizing and administration of the group while the others rotate jobs weekly. Their routine is fairly simple:

1　On Tuesday, the co-ordinator calls the distributor to find out the cost of each item and the best buys.
2　The members then place their orders and they are collated.
3　On Thursday, two members with station wagons arrive at the market to pay for the produce at 8:30 or 9 A.M., and the order is placed in their cars for them. If there is anything else that seems desirable when they are at the market, they have the liberty to pick that up as well.
4　When they arrive home, the house porter brings the crates to an apartment. The two shoppers, and the member whose apartment is being used that week, work together to weigh and package the food.
5　From 12 to 3 P.M., the two other members make up the individual orders and place the list for the coming week in each bag.
6　From 3:30 to 5:30 P.M., the apartment is open for members to pick up and pay for their orders.
7　The surplus is for sale to members who wish to add to their orders or to nonmember tenants in the building.

They find that their savings are greatest and difference in quality most apparent on perishable items. One member reported, "I am able to make great out-of-season buys. I still use the supermarket when I run out of fresh fruits and vegetables because we eat those in such large quantities."

In a country of individualists, busy with their own pursuits, it is surprising to see the enthusiasm and good will generated by these clubs. A typical small club that has been running quite successfully since 1970 started in the SoHo section of New York with twenty-four families.

Anna-Leah Braudes, a young, well-organized public relations woman, volunteered to be record-keeper. During the first two years, there were five jobs each week: driver, buyer, distributor (who furnishes the apartment or loft for this purpose), and two packers. The driver and buyer went to the Hunts Point terminal to select the produce and cheese, and then brought it to the designated loft or home of the week. It was the responsibility of the distribution person to be home when the buyers got there to receive the food. At 3 o'clock in the afternoon, the packers would arrive to divide the produce into twenty-four packages. There was usually a shopping bag and a half to be picked up between 5 and 7 o'clock. All for three dollars! A box of leftovers called "free" was also available for any of the members to choose from.

The distribution person collected the money and noted whether or not a member paid. Late payments had to be kept to a minimum. The money and the book were then passed to next week's team of driver and buyer.

The group had the usual two-year crisis, and instead of collapsing as most clubs do at this point, they decided to simplify, deciding that the jobs of packing and distributing were easier and should be combined. They finally worked out a more equitable team of three.

The club is still going strong, with occasional meetings and bulletins to work out any new problems. They are flexible enough to skip a week if the market is closed or if too many members are out of town. They also wanted more fruit and now pay six dollars for more than enough fruit, vegetables, and cheese to last the week. (Those six dollars will get you four feet down a supermarket aisle, but won't get you past the checkout counter with much.)

Anna-Leah has worked out some excellent methods of keeping records. The following are samples and items from bulletins that she has sent out.

ASSIGNMENT SHEET

1	Roman	Driver	Nov. 2, Dec. 7, Jan. 4
	Johns	Buyer	
	Long	Distribution & pickup	
2	Walker	Driver	Nov. 9, Dec. 14, Jan. 11
	White	Buyer	
	Reed	Distribution & pickup	

On Thursday, Nov. 23rd (Thanksgiving), the Hunts Point market is closed. Also the driver will be out-of-town that whole week, so—there will not be a co-op that week.

I will be glad to take all names submitted for our waiting list, but families or individuals with cars will have priority.

Please bring small bills (a five, a single and some change) when picking up your produce.

Buyers and Drivers may ask to have sealed crates of vegetables or fruits opened if they cannot see the contents.

Packers should avoid using plastic bags, as that raises costs.

The packer should have on hand several dozen small paper bags for packing small perishables, such as strawberries and/or mushrooms, *separately, on top*.

Remember, if some week you cannot carry out an assignment, it is your responsibility to provide a replacement for that week.

If you lose your assignment sheet, please call me (Telephone #)

A buyer in our cooperative needs to share half of her weekly vegetables. Please ask around for someone who would be interested in half a share.

If you have any suggestions as to how we could improve the selection of vegetables that we receive each week, please call me or leave a message at the next distribution point.

Each member also has a list of all the members, with names, telephone numbers, addresses, and function. If another member of a family is unable to undertake a task when required, it is easy enough to make a switch. They are relaxed and accommodate each other, yet are efficient and strict about cooperative responsibility.

A trip to the Hunts Point section of the Bronx, where the largest market in the United States is located, was exhilarating, even at 6 A.M. Josh Wolman was the driver and a new member, Madelone Jones, was the shopper that week. The parking was easy and soon they were walking through one of the four rows of stalls where crates of crisp asparagus and perfect artichokes were piled high. The wholesaler was friendly and curious as they stopped at one stall that had a good price on tomatoes.

Madelone had been keeping track of the prices on various stalls but Josh was still uncertain. The vendor cheerfully opened the crate. Uniformly firm, ripe tomatoes met immediate approval. At $3.50 for a thirty-pound bushel, they were a great buy when the same quality was selling for 69¢ a pound in the stores.

Josh did a double-take on his way past a huge stall filled with flower flats. It was the week before Easter and the potted plants were selling at less than one-third of the price in New York, and after a hurried consultation, they decided that it was too good to pass up. Thus the SoHo group enjoyed an occasional seasonal treat.

Some buying clubs say that the best food is gone by 6:30 in the morning, but there was still enough of everything these shoppers wanted. By 8 o'clock, they had everything in the back of the station wagon, including an extra crate of grapefruit for one of the members.

On the way home there was generally a good feeling of a job well done (and so early in the morning). Josh, who is also a research scientist in New Jersey, said, "I now eat less meat and I seldom go into a supermarket except for staples." He divides this membership with another single person and they share both the cost and the labor.

Undoubtedly, a chain store could command a lower wholesale price, but it is still worthwhile saving for the group.

This is how the $70 was distributed. The small balance went for gasoline. (See page 12.)

Even groups interested in natural foods have managed to cut the

Lettuce (Union)	(24)	$4.30
Artichokes	(24)	5.50
Broccoli	(14)	6.50
Tomatoes	(30 lbs.)	3.50
Navel oranges	(72)	5.25
Strawberries	(2 crates)	8.40
Bananas	(40 lbs.)	4.00
Grapefruit	(27)	5.00
Scallions	(36)	2.50
Squash	crate	5.50
Spinach	bushel	3.00
Flowers	(12)	7.00
Cheese	(12 lbs.)	8.40
	Total	$68.85

cost from 20 to 50% off regular store prices. In some areas where there is a demand, there are farmers that sell naturally grown food. (Unless there is an organization that does regular chemical testing, you have no proof that any organic food is truly chemical-free.) Clubs in many cities have made arrangements with health food stores or co-ops to buy in large quantities. Call various stores to check out prices and arrangements. Some stores do their own chemical testing as well.

For grains, nuts, and dried fruit a club should have a room with adequate work space, a sink, plastic bags, ladles, and a scale. Some member will probably have a retired baby scale available, and cut-up bleach bottles can serve as funnels and scoops. All the shoppers should bring their own premeasured jars for honey and peanut butter. Dry goods are generally purchased once a month and distributed at the same time as the produce. Unless the group is going to divide the entire purchase, cool, dry storage space is needed. Most clubs use new plastic garbage pails and liners with tight covers. Smaller quantities are kept in plastic jars. There is always some waste or uneven weighing, so a 2 to 5% markup is advised.

Cheese is a little more difficult to cut accurately and will have to be weighed and priced after cutting and wrapping. Some stores will do this for a small additional charge on large orders.

Many young people, and some not so young, have found still another solution to the high cost of living. Some are at the start of their careers, while others seek alternate lifestyles. Unconverted brownstone buildings in Brooklyn and Boston, as well as huge turn-of-the-century homes in other areas, have become cooperative houses. Unlike communes, the members work at jobs elsewhere and only share expenses and chores.

One group that ranges from 30 to 36 members in Boulder, Colorado, reported, "Our aim is to survive economically. Each person contributes ninety-five dollars a month for room, board, utilities, piano, and swimming pool." They buy sides of beef at a local shopping center, canned and frozen foods from a wholesaler in Denver, day-old bread from a bakery in Boulder, wholesale produce in Denver, and grains from a co-op. With all the members sharing the work, decisions, and expenses, it has become "a home rather than a rooming house."

Buying clubs also require the ability to plan ahead and order for the coming week. The food has to be promptly packaged and refrigerated at home. If they are to be kept for a week, salad greens, peas, string beans and carrots can be placed in plastic bags to maintain the moisture and fresh appearance of the vegetables.

Clubs do not compete with each other. Instead they are sometimes able to expand their range of items by joining for certain purchases. To prevent the loss of savings when food is unsold, the New York Department of Consumer Affairs recommends that you keep a list of people that are interested in buying the surplus of specialized items or large-scale purchases.

The following rules and procedures have evolved from the clubs that have survived their growing pains.

THE FIRST MEETING

A first meeting should be held with at least one member from each family present. Just how the buying club functions and what the limitations are should be explained, as well as the advantages. It is better to agree at the onset that the prime consideration is to be, say, economy, or a chance to buy strawberries in January and mushrooms at a moderate price, or a combination of such reasons. How does the group feel about boycotting lettuce or grapes? If it is a meat-buying club, do they want prime meat or are they looking for more economy? Are some in the group seeking a source of naturally grown food? That frequently comes higher in price, does not look as pretty as chemically treated produce, and may cause dissension unless some agreement is reached beforehand.

It should not come as a shock that each member has to share the work load and that the jobs are rotated. There should be a few members for each job: purchasing, distributing, driving (and placing crates into cars), and simple record-keeping. A work schedule is set up at this time, and a list of the types of produce should be drawn up with preferences and dislikes.

Usually between six and ten dollars will serve for a membership fee. That will cover the next week's purchases. If a member does not show up to collect the food, it should be agreed at this time that the fee is to be forfeited. Some groups add an extra fee for that contingency. If a member does not forfeit the fee by a failure to pick up the food, it is refunded when the member leaves the club.

If a member wishes to drop out, there should be a replacement. Two weeks' notice is generally time enough to find a new member from a waiting list and keep the continuity of the club.

If there is going to be a problem about child care, it should be discussed and sitters' services exchanged.

About a dollar is allotted to the driver, for expenses and toll fees if necessary.

SHOPPING HINTS

1 New shoppers should shop with experienced shoppers only.
2 Keep a weekly book for the shopper to check last week's prices.
3 Make cost per item calculations. (There are six pounds of mushrooms to a basket. At 89¢ a pound, it may not be a bargain. The buyer should have some idea of how the retail

prices have been running during the week. Check with local newspaper or USDA office.)

4 Check your list to see if an item is desirable or if perhaps enough was bought last week. (Onions do not have to be purchased each week.)

5 It is worth trying a few stalls to get comparative prices. After the shopper pays for the purchase, the price should be entered immediately into the book, and if the item is not put into the car at once, the receipt should be clipped onto a clipboard or entered in a book. You can organize the receipts by the stall number when it comes time to collect your purchases.

6 Do not be shy about asking the seller to open a crate if the contents are not readily visible.

7 Two shoppers are needed for a group of twelve. At least one should be strong enough to put the crates into the car (or persuasive enough to convince another to do it). Some items, like a crate of melons, may have to be handled by two people.

8 Record the weight or count of each purchase so that it can be divided later. Before the first shopping trip, the buyer should have an idea of what the group wants. Remember that if you buy a bushel of radishes for your co-op, you may end up with six bunches each for the week.

9 Local farmers' markets are frequently cheaper than distribution depots to which food has been shipped. Again, compare prices.

RECORD-KEEPING

This is one job that should not rotate often. It is best held by someone who cannot go to the market or do the distribution, and who has good organizational ability. The other jobs should be rotated and assignments made by the member who keeps the records. Some suggestions:

1 A list of members should be kept with their telephone numbers, as well as a reserve list of members. There should be enough members with cars or station wagons in the club to rotate, as well as members who can provide distribution space.
2 The next week's purchases are paid for when the food is picked up at the distribution point.
3 There is generally a little money left over to cover gasoline, tolls, paper expenses, and scales.
4 If there is an unexpected expense, the group generally places a 5% surcharge for a few weeks on the purchases.
5 Some memberships are shared by two single people, with food expenses and labor divided.

DISTRIBUTION

Lofts, large hallways, back porches, community rooms are ideal distribution centers. There are always some stray lettuce leaves and all those crates to be cleaned up. This is either handled by those responsible for dividing up the food or by the owner of the house.

The distribution people should, preferably, furnish the bags and cartons. Members should also bring a supply with them.

Many small buying clubs have a life span of about two years. The groups that are most successful are those whose members understand the necessity for cooperation and have a sense of responsibility to the group.

They seem to enjoy working together, and have fun. They have managed to follow a few rules and are rewarded by fresher food for less money.

The next chapter deals with the larger buying clubs, for those who would like to expand or affiliate with other groups.

chapter **3**

The Large Buying Club

The small, successful co-op buying club is frequently tempted to add to their membership and buying power. This is possible under certain circumstances if:

1 There is a nucleus of highly motivated members willing to undertake more responsibility and careful organization.
2 The new members understand the need of joint effort and the feeling of community that a cooperative effort requires.
3 There is another nearby co-op store or warehouse that the new group can affiliate with for stability, experience, and better wholesale prices.
4 The expansion is in stages. The co-op should not undertake more fixed expenses than the membership base will permit (use a garage or back yard if necessary at first). New types of food should be added only as fast as equipment and personnel can handle them efficiently.
5 There is a genuine need. The co-op should be able to offer better food at a cheaper price or food that is not obtainable in the area. The more successful co-ops have something more. While they cannot carry the 6000 items that a super-market does, they do have the warmth and friendliness that comes of working together for a common goal and without a profit motive.

Without these factors to start with, many groups have failed. What was an effective buying club, full of good hopes, can turn into one of those many small businesses that fail each year.

The items that a food co-op can offer are limited only by energy and imagination. In Austin, Texas, fish and shrimp are bought cooperatively, fresh from the boats. In Michigan, a peanut.butter manufacturer agreed to fresh grind co-op peanuts, producing the finest peanut better in Michigan. Other possibilities include: vegetables, fruits, eggs, milk, honey, grains, oils, nuts, and yogurt. Even canned goods can be obtained, but most co-ops find that they cannot buy them cheaper than the large food chains. They usually discontinue carrying them unless they have enough volume to enable them to buy competitively. This also requires storage space.

What all the successful clubs have in common is excellent organization and the willingness to work together. Some affiliate with an existing co-op store; others prefer to remain small and independent.

Some groups call themselves "Food Conspiracies" and many grew without the knowledge that others, in all parts of the country, were attempting the same experiment.*

Biographies of a few large buying groups follow. Much can be learned from all their histories, even those with problems.

FREE VENICE CO-OP
440 Venice Way
Venice, California 90291

The Free Venice Co-op is so well organized a co-op without a permanent "home" or paid staff that they have served as a model for many others. They started small, operating out of back yards and garages in 1970. Now they use the backroom of a friendly store as their weekly distribution point for most of their foods. Before long they hope to have the use of a Parks Department warehouse to combine all their activities. Meanwhile the 180 members are able to save about 50% on produce, bread, cheese, and other staples. They no longer buy dairy products because they found that the savings were minimal.

A Newport Beach family supplies freshly caught fish for some of

*A small group exists in Philadelphia with the purpose of promoting the idea and aiding those interested.

the members and through a coalition of similar Los Angeles co-ops they are able to order about $700 a month of health food staples.

After a meeting of other California co-ops held in Fresno in the summer of 1972, they brought back the idea of team structure that they are now using. One member has been able to use his experience with computers to print out an equitable and efficient work schedule.

Their library team reports that:

> Decisions are made at the weekly meetings by the members. Often members keep us abreast of relevant matters in the Venice community, and sometimes we join together in some activity beyond the co-op. (We have twice elected representatives to the Venice Health Council.)

While they are able to save about half of the supermarket or health food store prices, they find that members have additional reasons for belonging to the Free Venice Co-op:

> We get to know and work with our neighbors and friends. We are maintaining a social model in which the incentive to work is not money, but love. We are experimenting with more democratic work relationships. We promote the idea of cooperation action, and act as a base for further cooperation. We choose our food (e.g., UFWOC, not Teamster lettuce). We get some foods (Tamari, raw honey, natural teas) hard to find in regular stores. We support whom we choose, e.g., small organic farmers. Many of us get almost all our food through the co-op, and hardly enter a store anymore.

The members range from secretaries, teachers, dancers, professors, poets, mechanics, lawyers to mothers and "hippies." There are many members who are in their seventies who also find a place in the co-op.

They cover the waste costs and small expenses by using a 10% markup on staples and 5% markup, plus ten cents per adult head tax on produce.

There is much to be learned by their procedures, which are

described at the end of this chapter in the section "How a Large Buying Club Works." The co-op also welcomes any inquiries and offers help to those who wish to set up their own.

V.O.I.C.E. Co-op
2 Shattuck Street
Nashua, New Hampshire 03060

This buying club started in May, 1971, as part of a joint project between VOICE, a grass-roots low-income group, and SHARE, a group of middle-class citizens interested in low-income problems. Together they started out with 14 or 15 families, and combined purchases with the Manchester, New Hampshire, Co-op. The order was large enough to make it worthwhile for the Manchester coordinator to make the trip and the VOICE Co-op paid him a 10% markup on the order.

Having started out buying only fruits and vegetables, the co-op now sells grains, dairy products, bread, eggs, and some organic foods, in addition to produce. Members save at least 15% to 20% on what they buy. Among the co-op's wholesalers and suppliers is the New England Food Cooperating Organization (NEFCO).

Their location has changed several times; at the present they work out of a large room or wing of a community house which once was a school. Their work plan has also undergone changes since they found a need for more organization as the co-op grew. Originally one or two people handled everything but distribution. Now they have an inner core of 15 workers, a few of whom take on heavy responsibilities. All members must work at least two hours every month.

VOICE buys with the Manchester and Milford Co-ops. They rent a U-Haul; the trucker is paid through VISTA. "If he [the trucker] goes, we adjust. There is a strong will to keep going." This buying club has three part-time workers paid through Community Action Plans.

Membership has now reached some 80 families. With the exception of the lettuce controversy, the group has remained apolitical, thus making the co-op available to conservative and liberal or radical members. "Some buy with us because they like control

over *how* and *what* they buy. Others because they save money. It's
the acceptance of many opinions that keeps the co-op worth using."

THE ITHACA REAL FOOD CO-OP
P.O.Box 871
Ithaca, New York 14850

One of the larger food-buying groups without a paid staff or rent,
this group began in the spring of 1971. It had been a "food conspiracy" in the back of a local bookstore, distributing grains, honey,
flour, oil, and other foods. Originally there was a 10% markup to
cover trucking and other expenses and an optional fee to join. Although there were 300 memberships (about a thousand people), it
was not a true cooperative venture. One member, Peter Orville, said,
"Only a few people did the work while the others left the place a mess
and treated it like a supermarket. We got discouraged and when the
store closed welcomed the chance to reorganize."

They held a meeting at which about a hundred people turned up,
and started the Ithaca Real Food Co-op. After much debate they
decided on a format without a store. Instead they decided to decentralize into a few cooperating regions. At first there was just a city and
a country region, followed soon after by a college town region.

Today, there are 24 regions of three to forty members each. They
are roughly divided into five for the city, twelve in the surrounding
30-mile rural area, six for the college area, and one for a housing
complex. The 500-family membership is varied and includes the
local public school principal. Because of this they are able to use the
school gym for distribution of produce and some dairy products. The
members range from students, residents of the local community, poor
people of all ages (but very few blacks). There was an effort to start a
"region" in the downtown black community, but it did not prosper.
Occasionally there is an order from members of the local welfare-
rights organization.

Each group has its own bookkeeper who organizes and runs the
region, from a week to several months at a time, before handing the
job on. The routine is roughly the same as in any buying club:

1 The individual turns in an order with payment and any credit from previous weeks to the bookkeeper on Tuesday evening.
2 The bookkeeper brings the total regional order form to the central meeting on Wednesday evening.
3 Orders are compiled and buyers go to Syracuse on Saturday morning.
4 Food is brought to the gym and distributed to the region representatives.
5 Food is trucked to a regional members' home and broken down into individual orders.

Peter says, "This all takes a good deal of work and each member puts in a few hours a month, *if at all possible*. Some people work more than others." They have put together a manual of operations to take the guesswork out of each job and to co-ordinate efforts.

The co-op does not have a formal "board" but has control jobs instead. The jobs are: two bookkeepers, three or four central buyers, two grain supervisors, a produce distributor, a credit supervisor, a central meeting "clerk," a newsletter writer, and regional bookkeepers.

Policy is usually made at the Wednesday night meetings by all who are present. Orders are collated at this meeting, and Peter says, "Buyers for the week are chosen or 'coaxed.' Major changes seem to evoke negative responses from the most active workers, while minor changes leading to greater efficiency are welcomed." The original conspiracy charged a $2 membership fee; the new co-op does not. They had $7000 left over from the former organization which was used to buy stock and to set up a bank account to pay for produce.

They have kept a 10% markup for produce to cover the trucking and spoilage, but sell the cheese, bread, and grains at cost. The co-op has an extensive list of items, and when they are unable to obtain a few they offer a refund. The members are aware of the difficulty of obtaining a full order and complaints are rare. One member said, "Even when you go to a regular store you can't always get everything you want."

After realistically handling the problems that required organization, they are now faced with a difficulty many isolated co-ops have: the need for cooperative wholesale operations. The Ithaca group looks forward to a day when co-ops throughout the New England, New York, and Pennsylvania areas can combine forces. They would like to be able to get direct shipment of a boxcar or two of produce to be divided among the co-ops. And they would like to hear from other co-ops who would like to investigate this idea. The main source of information for the co-op is the storefront on West State Street in Ithaca. This is a center for welfare rights, tenant rights, and other community activities. Many different people use the storefront, although it is funded and mostly staffed by the Human Affairs Program at Cornell University.

PEOPLE BUYING TOGETHER, INC.
222 Varsity Circle
Arlington, Texas 76010

This food corporation, which services co-ops in and around Dallas, Texas, was started in May, 1970, by a few families and individuals loosely associated through Southern Methodist University in Dallas. They pooled their food needs (mostly produce) to buy in bulk at the municipal farmer's market. This basic idea spread among friends and acquaintances, and thus the co-op was formed. (One of the founders had received his co-op training in the Peace Corps.)

As interest grew among people in other areas, People Buying Together incorporated in November, 1970, as a regional organization to co-ordinate bookkeeping and buying for the original Dallas co-op and its offshoots. Today there are nine local co-ops: six in Dallas and one each in Arlington, Fort Worth, and Denton.

The local co-ops of this large buying club utilize space in community centers, churches, and homes; all work is done on a volunteer basis. Orders are collected by the local co-ops during the week and are pooled to form a master buying list. The food is then purchased on Saturdays and distributed to members on the same day.

There is a 10% markup (5% to PBT, 5% to local co-ops for expenses) on a wide selection of fresh produce, as well as organic foods, dairy products, and bread. Bread is handled merely as a convenience since there is no real saving on this item compared with thrift stores. Meat is not sold due to strict city, state, and federal regulations; storage also presents problems.

Due to the regional makeup of PBT, it is hard to estimate the number of members. The Arlington co-op is the largest with 60 to 70 memberships, while the smallest in East Dallas may have 10 members. Each membership may be an individual, a family, or any number of people. Roger Pierce of the Arlington co-op estimates that PBT, Inc. has a total of 250 memberships, reaching 700 to 1000 people. Young people and those connected with a school constitute about 50 to 60% of total membership.

PBT has had some failures in organizing in minority communities, and as a result membership is predominantly white (80 to 90%). The aims of its members range from the idealistic to the practical, i.e., cheap food.

HOW A LARGE BUYING CLUB WORKS

The following organization plan is suitable for a collection of buying groups without a "home." (They use the back of a friendly store.)

This is the orientation booklet supplied to new members of the Free Venice Co-op in California. It is broken down in such a manner to facilitate their quick absorption into the group.

In addition, this group also uses the "team system" so that each operation does not depend on one member.

Individual Responsibilities

MEMBERSHIP

1 Each Co-op member must work a minimum of 4 hours each month. This includes each adult in a large household and also those people who do not order each week.

2 Each Co-op member deposits the approximate amount of money they spend on produce each week. ($5.00 or multiple thereof) before first order.

3 Returning Co-op members who have already paid buying

deposit (membership fee) will be allowed to order. Because back records over a year old are nonexistent these deposits will not be refundable.

ORDERING AND PAYING

1 A reasonable effort shall be made by all Co-op workers to see that any members receive food who place an order and who, in good faith, make a reasonable effort to abide by the rules of the Co-op.
2 Members pay a surcharge of 10% of the cost of the order plus 10¢ per adult in a household (head tax). This money will be used to cover expenses, losses due to spillage, etc.
3 Co-op does not accept I.O.U.'s—ask another member for a personal loan.

PRODUCE

1 All produce order sheets must be submitted by 9:00 P.M. Tuesday through meetings or team co-ordinators. All the blanks on the order should be completely filled out.
2 Unpicked up orders: one call will be made to orderer, then food will be sold as extra with a 10% ($1.00 minimum) charge to orderer.

STAPLES

1 50¢ charge for late pickups.
2 Orders not picked up at distribution point will be kept one week with an additional 10% ($1.00 minimum) charge.

Team Responsibilities

1 One member from each produce team must be at each Tuesday night meeting. One member from each staples team must be at the 1st Tuesday meeting of the month (Staples Ordering night).
2 Team co-ordinator does not have to perform actual manual labor—applies to any team that feels their co-ordinator is putting in a lot of hours for Co-op.

Co-op Responsibilities

1 All payments and expenses are to be brought up before Co-op for approval and confirmation.
2 Co-op is bound to refund membership to departing member. Only Treasury Team is authorized to refund membership fee.
3 Decisions are made by majority vote at meetings. At this point, there is no official quorum. Nonattending members abdicate decision-making power.

Etiquette

1 Share equally. Not to try for personal gain at other's expense, e.g., pick over food.
2 Be understanding. Mistakes happen. Correct, don't blame. The Co-op is a learning experience.
3 Take time to be actively concerned with Co-op—not just getting job done as quickly as possible.
4 Meetings: Share time, don't take more than your share. Don't preach, yell, condescend. Quiet people have good ideas too. Don't use meeting as a captive audience.
5 Do favors if asked, e.g., pick up other's order.
6 If you suggest new work, be ready to volunteer.
7 Packing team should distribute food evenly. Share shortages.
8 Be responsible.

How To Order and Buy

Produce order sheets should be available at the weekly meeting, and perhaps at produce distribution. (They are periodically revised and reprinted by the Library Team.) When you get one, fill in all the information at the top: "living group" means name of household or commune, or last name of people ordering; phone # where storekeeper can reach you, e.g., if you forget to pick up; team (if you don't have a team yet, see the Orientation person); "date last worked"—if you just joined, write "new."

You are now ready to order your food. Notice that some foods are ordered by the pound (zucchini, mushrooms, corn, broccoli). A pound is about 2-3 apples or oranges, 2-4 avocados, 4-5 bananas, whole lotta garlic. Keep in mind that not everything ordered is likely to come, and to order slightly more than you will need. Some items will not come at all; the highly seasonal items especially (stoned fruit, asparagus) may be too expensive or too inedible to buy. Some items will be purchased in an amount less than our order, so that we can buy whole crates and not have an inconvenient amount left as surplus.

If you want something that isn't on the order sheet, write it clearly in the blank spaces provided. If you know where the Shoppers can get it, include that information. Delivery is not guaranteed.

In order to be tallied, order sheets must be collected at the meeting on Tuesday by 9 P.M. Talliers will collect them there; late orders are too much hassle. If you can't get your order sheet to the meeting without help, phone your team coordinator.

Your food should be waiting for you at the produce distribution site during the hours of pickup. If you come too early, you will have to wait or help pack. (Food can't be taken until paid for. The storekeeper isn't ready until the prices are done, and *all* the orders are packed.)

Get your order sheet from the storekeeper. (They should be in alphabetical order.) Find a number circled on your order sheet. Then find your box of food with the same number in order on the shelves. Your name should be written on the box. Make sure you get all the boxes with your number on it.

Check your food against the order sheet. "Get own" means take what you ordered from the stash that's around somewhere (sometimes cheese or juice or eggs). If packers made a mistake, ask storekeeper if you can correct it.

Remember: shortages are shared, and not everything ordered is likely to come.

When you have gotten your order, look around to see if there is anything else available that you want. There may be bread in boxes near the storekeeper. The shoppers may have bought a crate of surprise. Surplus may be on the floor (after all the orders are filled, what remains is available on a first-come, first-serve basis). Don't pick out the best whatevers and leave the worst for the rest of us. If something is rotten, throw it away, and take a fair share of the rest. If you buy anything you didn't order, mark it in the last section of the order sheet, and add it in with your order.

Prices should be marked on the price chart, which should be hanging in plain sight. (Prices are calculated from the cost per crate, and are rounded upwards to the nearest whole cent.) Copy onto your order sheet the price of each item you got, multiply by quantity to get cost, and add. Transfer the total to the appropriate blank at the top of the order sheet. Fill in the surcharge blank (total cost + 10% currently), and "head tax" (currently 10¢ for each adult in household eating the food). Add together, and pay storekeeper.

The surcharge and head tax are used to pay the overhead: expenses such as gas for the truck, bags, and ditto paper; and losses such as rotten tomatoes, spilled bean sprouts, or dropped apple juice. (Head tax is sometimes called "rent"; it was once earmarked for that purpose.)

After you have bought your co-op food (or while waiting to get it) look around the stores. Harold usually has inexpensive cheeses, Alta Dena Dairy products (for co-op members he will match supermarket price), cookies and cakes, sometimes toilet paper. Our distribution site is rent-free; all Harold asks is some business.

If for any reason you can't pick up your food, and can't find a friend to pick it up for you, by all means *telephone* store as soon as possible, definitely before 6 P.M. Thursday. The co-op has fronted all our money for your food, confident that you will purchase it on schedule. We have had severe losses at times when orders were not picked up. Currently, orders not picked up are declared surplus shortly after 6 P.M. unless some arrangement has been made, and the orderer must pay a discouragement fee of $1 or 10%.

Team Descriptions—Produce

TALLYING

Date: Tuesday night or Wednesday during day.
Time: 9:00 P.M. Tuesday + 2 hours.
Place: Weekly meeting + home of team member.

At the Tuesday night meeting collect produce orders and master order sheets. Arrange with shopper of the week to deliver the tally to him by Wednesday evening. Then:

1 List on the master order sheet a grand total of how much of each item is ordered.
2 Phone egg orders to Harold before 4:00 P.M. Wednesday.
3 Make packing slips for cheese and mushrooms.
4 Alphabetize and number the order sheets. Write out a list of the orders for the storekeeper.

This job is usually done by two people per week.

SHOPPING

Date: Thursday morning.
Time: 3:00-6:30 A.M.
Place: Terminal and City Markets, Downtown L.A.

The shopping team spends between $300.00 and $800.00 of the cooperative's money each and every week. It is our responsibility to see that the cooperative gets its money's worth, not just cheap vegetables quickly bought, but the best low-cost food available carefully selected. We determine that the grocery value received is equal to the grocery dollar spent.

Produce is bought every Thursday morning between the hours of 3:00 and 6:30 A.M. by two or more shoppers. The shoppers have a list of preferable stalls where the co-op has shopped before at which we can compare taste, price, and quality. At present the shoppers have been authorized to spend an additional $10.00 on unordered food we think will be interesting to co-op members.

After shopping, the truckers meet us at the market at 6:30 A.M. We turn over the produce receipts, the master shopping list, the individual order sheets and the cooperative Log Book. The shopping team retains the cashbox and brings it to the distribution site later that day (when produce is picked up) for the treasurer. The shoppers should be home no later than 7:30 A.M.

TRUCKING
> Date: Thursday morning.
> Time: Arrive downtown at 6:00 A.M., distribution point (the store) at 9:00 A.M.
> Place: Terminal and City Markets, Downtown L.A., to distribution point.

The truckers' job is to pick up the food at the downtown produce market and transport it to the distribution point.

They meet the shoppers in the restaurant or cafe next door to pick up all the receipts for produce and the paperwork for the prepacking team. To pick up produce the truckers proceed counterclockwise around the market—one person drives, one deals with the stallkeepers, and one loads the food. They then take the produce to the distribution point and help unload the truck.

The trucking team is in need of a truck.

PRODUCE PREPACKAGING
> Date: Thursday.

Time: 9:00 A.M.-4:00 P.M.
Place: Produce distribution site, currently the store.

Produce Prepackaging is done all day on Thursdays from 9:00
A.M., when the truck arrives from downtown with the produce at the distribution point, until 4:00 P.M., when the
storekeepers arrive and the food distribution begins.

Usually members of the prepackaging team work in 2 hour
shifts every other week to complete their 4 hour per month
minimum work requirement.

The two main responsibilities of the job are to help the
truckers unload the produce from the truck and accurately fill
the produce orders, with any shortages evenly distributed
among the orders. The team prepackages items such as cheese
and mushrooms by weighing them according to the prepackaging slips. The other items in each order are boxed according
to an averaging system which eliminates weighing each item
for each order.

BREAD PICK-UP
     Date: Every Thursday.
     Time: Before 4:00 P.M.
     Place: Bread source to produce distribution site.

About half an hour before produce pickup on Thursday go to
Good Stuff Bakery on West Washington and pick up bread.
Amount varies, the people at Good Stuff can tell you the
current amount. Also get some cakes and muffins. Sign
receipt and be sure it's marked "Not Paid." Take bread,
cakes, and muffins to pickup site before pickup starts and give
receipt to storekeeper. All told, takes about 1 hour a week.

STOREKEEPING
     Date: Thursday.
     Time: 4:00-6:45 P.M.

Place: Produce Distribution Site, currently the store.

Fascinating job for all interested in human psychology and behavior. Requires a clear brain, quickness and accuracy with numbers and money and tolerance for a sometimes hectic situation.

Be present at distribution point before store opens (before 4:00 P.M.). First task is to see that all orders have been packed, prices of food displayed, and surplus food supply made visible. The storekeeper opens store with the supply of money duly counted, greets the members genially, and explains procedures to new members. When members are ready to make payment storekeeper goes over order form to see if it is correct and makes change. It is co-op policy that storekeeper not accept I.O.U.'s. At 6:00 P.M. storekeeper calls all those who have not picked up to remind them. After 6:30 adds up cash receipts and totals all monies. Puts all receipts of food purchased and master sheets in cashbox.

The storekeeper must be prepared to settle hassles of members disgruntled about food not received and help the treasury team watch for losses.

PRODUCE CLEANUP
  Date: Thursday.
  Time: 5:30-7:00 P.M.
  Place: Produce Distribution Site, currently the store.

Two team members arrive at store approximately 30 minutes before closing (5:30 P.M.).

1 Sweep up and mop the floor.
2 Haul away all excess boxes which cannot be used for the next week's prepackaging.
3 Haul away garbage.
4 Weigh all extra produce and make 2 lists with costs (1 for Harold and 1 for treasurer).

CLOSE-UP

    Date: Thursday.

    Time: 6:00-7:30 P.M.

    Place: Produce Distribution Site, currently the store.

Go at 6:00. Say hello to Harold, he's usually glad to know someone's there to watch his store. Purchase groceries. If everyone else has purchased groceries, relieve shopkeeper and keep an eye on the cashbox. Cleanup crew is usually there. Stay at front of store to discourage people from coming in while cleanup crew is working—tell them store is closed. When cleanup is completed turn off lights in back room and in the refrigerator. Take cashbox and order sheets. Lock store with someone from cleanup crew. Hop in car and go to Produce Treasurer's. Give him cashbox and order sheets. Usually this takes a good 1-1-1/2 hours. Get home at 7 to 7:30.

Team Descriptions—Staples

ORDER TAKING

    Date: First Tuesday of each month.

    Time: 7:30-9:30 P.M.

    Place: Meeting site, currently pavillion card room.

This team collects money and orders for the monthly staples distribution.

1 Put some original change in the cashbox; write down this amount for treasurer.
2 Make numbers to give to people as they give you their orders.
3 Check arithmetic on each order. Write OK, or correct the total.
4 Call out number of orders in turn. For each order, collect the money, and write down the form of payment (cash, check, stamps, credits).

Four people on this team are sufficient.

CONTAINERS

Date: First Tuesday of each month, and as needed for a week and a half.

Time: 7:30-9:30 P.M. and as needed.

Place: Meeting site. (Staples distribution site, currently in Brentwood.)

This team makes sure that an adequate supply of containers is available for the Breakup and Packing teams to pack food. Containers are gathered at the staples ordering meeting, and perhaps at other designated times and places. Team also supplies bags and boxes, purchased or otherwise acquired. Packing slips or staples orders must be checked to be sure that the supply of containers is sufficient. Sometimes this job includes making a run to the Barrington Co-op recycling depot to gather more jars.

Team requires one or two people with a vehicle.

COMPILING

Date: First Wednesday after the first Tuesday of each month. (Maybe Thursday.)

Time: Whenever. Takes 2 people maybe 4 hours.

Place: Anywhere, usually home.

The Staples Compiling Team totals all the items on all the monthly staples orders in order to get our co-op's Master Order to Westside Cooperatives. This team also calculates the total cost, and makes instruction slips for the prepackers telling them how many packages of what quantities to make for each item. The hours are flexible and you can do it at home—a good job for people with small children.

BUYING

Date: Thursday following the first Tuesday of each month, and as needed.

Time: 7:30-10:00 P.M. and as needed.

Place: Westside   Meeting   Site   (currently   in   Brent-
         wood); where needed.

The Venice Co-op is a member of the Westside Co-ops,
which consists of about six co-ops similar to Venice. Staples
are purchased each month through the Westside Co-ops. Each
co-op within the Westside Co-ops sends one or more representatives to the buyer's meeting, which is held at 7:30 P.M.
on the Thursday following the Tuesday meeting at which the
staples orders are collected. At this meeting, staples buying
tasks are assigned to the various buyers from the individual
co-ops. Sometimes the assigned task involves only phoning
orders in to distributors. Sometimes the task includes being at
the staples distribution point to receive the order when it is
delivered. Since Venice has the largest order of all the co-ops
in the Westside Co-ops, the Venice buyer generally is given
the task of taking responsibility for the orders which have to
be picked up from the distributors. This generally has involved picking up a dry milk order in Commerce and a honey
order in Pasadena.

This team requires about two people and a vehicle.

BREAKUP
Date: The second Thursday after the first Tuesday of each
         normal month.
Time: About 7 P.M. until maybe 10:00, maybe 12:00.
Place: Westside Breakup Site, currently in Brentwood.

Staples Breakup is a good team for people who work days
because it all happens on a Thursday evening. The job consists of helping to subdivide the Westside Co-op food into the
shares of the various co-ops, and then to check that our share
was correctly done. We are also responsible for whatever
surplus remains. This is a good job for new members in that it
requires little specialized knowledge, involves meeting people   from   co-ops   all   over   western   L.A.,   and   gives

a sense of the magnitude of the whole staples operation. An advantage peculiar to this team is that members get first chance to buy surplus.

This team needs 4 to 8 people.

PACKING

Date: Second weekend after the first Tuesday of each month.
Time: Mostly daytime.
Place: Staples Distribution Site, currently in Brentwood.

Work all your hours at once. Choose your home (4 hours) once a month, either on Friday or Saturday. Grab a bag and a packing card and weigh out the orders. Late Saturday packers get to fill individual orders into boxes. This is a good team for new members in that little specialized knowledge is required.

The Staples Packing Co-ordinator sees that everything is GO for packing staples; calls team for work over a two day period, notes food received, shortages and extras, and keeps track of who works.

STOREKEEPING

Date: "Staples Sunday," the second Sunday after the first Tuesday of the month.
Time: About 9:45 until 1:45 P.M.
Place: Staples Distribution Site, currently in Brentwood.

The staples storekeeper must be at the distribution point by 10 A.M. on distribution day. The treasurer turns over the money box and receipt book to the storekeeper at that time. During the distribution time (10:00 A.M. to 1:00 P.M.) it is the responsibility of the storekeepers to see to it that each person picking up an order does the following:

1 Turns in his or her order form.
2 Lists the items on the back of the order form which were

ordered but not received (i.e., shortages), with the prices and total credit due.

3 Lists all the items purchased from surplus, and the total cost.

The storekeepers then either collect the amount owed or write a credit slip for the amount of credit owed the member. It is generally best to have two storekeepers, although in a pinch the job can be done by one person. One of the storekeepers must return the money box, receipt book, and order sheets to the treasurer.

CLEANUP

Date: Staples Sunday.
Time: 1-5 P.M.
Place: Staples Distribution Site, currently in Brentwood.

The Cleanup Team hauls away garbage, and makes the distribution site presentable. It is responsible for cataloging the remaining surplus, and putting it away in a large container. Two inventory lists of the surplus are made; one is left in the surplus container, and the other is brought to the Staples Treasurer, along with any staples orders which were not picked up.

This team needs 2 or 3 people to spend 3 or 4 hours; it is best to have two vehicles such as a station wagon or van.

Team Descriptions-Additional

TREASURY

Date: Thursday, and as needed.
Time: As needed, mostly flexible.
Place: Mostly at home.

The job of accounting for the co-op's money at present has

foci: the overall treasury, the inorganic treasury, and the staples treasury. The three jobs are as follows:

1 The staples treasurer: (a) checks to see if the money (food stamps, checks, and credits) received by the receiver equals the amount of food ordered; (b) compares these numbers with the staples order master; (c) prays that the breakup team will list the surplus and shortages of Free Venice Co-op and that cleanup will inventory the surplus left to be returned to Westside. With all this information the treasurer figures the check to Westside Cooperative. The treasurer also tries to keep track of credits issued to our members.
2 The inorganic treasurer prepares the money boxes for the buyers and the pickup. After pickup he collects all the money, bills, notes, and orders to produce a balance sheet about the treasury, then presents it to the overall treasurer to bring the buying fund to a standard amount (now at 500).
3 The overall treasurer writes the checks and makes the deposits and carries a double entry system for accounting of why the co-op has or does not have money. This treasurer also checks the other treasurers in their work. All the treasurers make checks at various points in the process to find weaknesses and to see in detail what is happening.

COMMUNICATION/LIBRARY

The co-op shares work among its many members, rather than concentrating it in the hands of store owner and employees. This decentralization of work and decision-making creates a substantial need for communication.

Our job is to see that need filled. We are responsible for publications such as order sheets, the weekly newsletter, membership lists, an orientation package. We also operate a co-op information phone, maintain correspondence with other co-ops, and occasionally provide publicity. We are in the process of organizing the co-op archives. Some of us have particular assignments: orient new members, maintain the work chart at the store, provide legal defense.

Some of our work is scheduled (e.g., take notes at meetings); much consists of projects to be done anywhere, anytime. Our tasks are as extensive as our imaginations. We have managed to accomplish our basic tasks; with more help we could undertake a variety of useful projects. We mostly work more than the 4 hour/month minimum (plus time at meetings).

chapter 4

The New Co-op Stores and Storefronts

The series of profiles in this chapter illustrates an important stage in the evolution of the co-op idea; the crucial moment when many small- to middle-sized buying clubs feel the need for a physical plant, premises from which to carry on their co-op buying and distributing.

For many of the clubs, the acquisition of a store or a storefront that could be kept open either full- or part-time was a step forward in scale. Several of the groups described here, flowered into allied activities. Some stayed strictly pro-economy stores; others gradually took on the aspect of a community center in which problems and ideas were exchanged, as well as inexpensive food was bought and sold. The co-ops became centers in which the symbolic value of food was a launching point into social, ecological, and political values.

Some groups found it more to their advantage to stay open only part-time—several hours a day, or several days a week. But in most cases, the move from a loosely organized buying club, with all the structural problems that arise from working without a physical base, to actual store, was felt by the members to be a positive step.

But it was not always a logical step. Some co-ops were under-capitalized, run by hopeful but inexperienced members, with margins that were too small to enable them to survive the unexpected calamities. The need was primarily for comfort, camaraderie, and a home away from home, rather than inexpensive food. For others it was truly the next logical step. They found that with a little tighter operation and some business sense they could still keep their ideals.

This "territorial imperative" is proof that an idea must have a home. And with that home the diversity of directions taken is extraordinary.

A great many of the new co-ops are set up as natural and organic food co-ops, or include such foods as a part of their merchandise. These people are concerned about the quality of life as well as a desire for economy.

Every few months there are new revelations from the Food and Drug Administration that a particular food additive must be removed because of some previously unknown side effect, or that some water supplies are contaminated by crop sprays. The Switchboard* in New York reports about their concern that the giant "agri-business" now wields such great power that it can prevent protective legislation until the damage is irreversible.

The well-organized members of California's co-op supermarkets have joined together through their individual cooperative organization to bring pressure on government agencies for more effective consumer protection. Through their Associated Cooperative they maintain a membership in the Cooperative League of the U.S.A. to try to increase consumer-oriented activities.

Others, in New York, Wisconsin, California, and elsewhere are seeking out the small farmers, especially those who use organic methods as a source of more natural food. Their purpose is twofold:

1 To help small farmers—many of them college graduates turning hopefully to a simpler life, others attempting to keep small family farms—maintain their land;
2 To find a cheaper direct source of food without the added expense of a middleman. For example, there is a newly formed organization for poor farmers in Georgia that ships organically raised food directly to co-op stores and depots.

Unfortunately, the health food business is too tempting a source of

*Switchboard is a collectively run, information center staffed by volunteers. Founded independently in many cities, each group attempts to connect people with the help that they need. The Switchboards have extensive contacts with various community such as: food co-ops, organic farmers, health care, employment and alcoholic treatment centers, housing and tenants' rights organizations. They also may provide lists of various social and political events. Some have emergency housing for runaways or a "hot line" for those who need help during a bad drug experience.

large profits for many packagers and farmers. The profit margin is so large in health food stores that co-ops are able to show the greatest savings for their members in that area. Many health food co-ops now do their own testing for chemical residuals or inspect the farms that are sources of food or meat.

Even with the controversy continuing as to whether or not it is possible to raise truly organic food, many co-ops members want to buy food that has been naturally raised with a minimum of chemical exposure.

The health food co-ops are frequently organized as small stores. They vary in style and operations, but they all have another function for their members. They serve some as a sanctuary of goodwill and fellowship; for others they are a place to form a better community or a means of extending family relations in a strange city.

While the majority of the members may be students or people seeking an alternate lifestyle, many are middle-class and elderly people in the community. The Wild Rice Co-op in New York reported that some Moslem and Orthodox Jewish members have become friendly on the basis of their dietary habits and the need to find other protein sources.

Whether the interest is primarily dietary control, purer food, or economic relief from supermarket prices, co-ops bring people together to find mutual solutions. Once started, the development of the co-op idea—from buying club to storefront to the formation of a large regional warehouse serving many co-ops—illustrates the transformation of a grass-roots idea into a nationwide cooperative movement. The following descriptions of individual co-ops show the evolution of the co-op idea.

COMMON MARKET OF COLORADO
1100 Champa
Denver, Colorado 80204

The Common Market is the only genuine cooperative food store in Denver. It was formed in February of 1971 and has become the parent organization for other such ventures in the area, offering advice, buying services, and discounts. This co-op started with some students at the University of Denver and a loan of $2000 from the student senate. They used very little of the loan at first since they shared a store with another co-op, and used a preorder form and a prepayment structure.

The store, which is open 3-1/2 days a week, is staffed by two full-time workers and one part-timer. They try to keep a 10% markup over cost. In certain cases there are selective markups, in which they choose to lose a penny in order to compete with local supermarkets. This is a close-to-the-bone markup, but Kathy de Paola of Common Market reports that they have established a firm financial base via Certificates of Deposit from the members. This capital has enabled them to grow into a true store and to bring their volume to $6000 to $7000 weekly. She advises others to consider this method.

Common Market's 600 active membership families represent the community to a large degree. Kathy credits this to the elimination of the order-form structure which requires the ability to read and to understand forms. As she says, "It is important to us to make sure our co-op has very little middle-class bias." They also carry a broad selection of foods: canned foods, meat, produce, grains, and health foods. She says, "We should not dictate what other people's habits ought to be—but should expose them to good foods, instead."

Common Market welcomes inquiries and can be a good source from which to locate other newly formed co-ops.

SUNFLOWER NATURAL FOODS STORE, INC.
1549 Main Street
Sarasota, Florida 33577

This cooperatively owned natural food store was opened in January, 1971, by two students. It has over 500 members in "one of the strongest Nixon counties (over 80%) in the nation." Half of the membership are students, the rest drawn from the community. This co-op has a paid professional staff of ten workers who receive minimal salaries.

The co-op is owned proportionally by its members. Each member owns a share equal to the amount purchased each month; thus the investment is shared proportionally. Members may purchase amounts equal to monthly deposits. (A $10 deposit enables you to buy up to $10 worth of goods a month.) Markup is 20% for members and 50% for nonmembers.

Sunflower Natural Foods is a now incorporated, "fully insured, and on good terms with local health officials." The store maintains an extensive stock of grains, flours, nuts, oils, dried fruits, herbs, spices, teas, meats, and confections. All items conform to the Organic Merchants' standards of no sugar, refined oil, or white flour, and almost everything is organically grown. The co-op also sells honey, eggs, and organic citrus which they buy from local farmers. But the Sunflower group will not sell any vitamins or cosmetics.

EARTH FOODS, INC. (trade name: EARTHWORKS)
1310-1312 West Main Street
Urbana, Illinois 61801

Earthworks began as a crafts store in November, 1969. Legally, it was a partnership with each of the five partners contributing $200 as a capital investment. The partners ran the store on their own, selling craft goods on consignment. Although some craft supplies were sold, the inventory basically consisted of homemade items.

Then Earth Foods opened in the spring of 1970, working out of the second storefront in the same building as Earthworks. This, too, was a partnership, in legal terms. However, funds were raised through the sale of $5 memberships, of which some 200 were sold. Selling only natural food dry goods (in bulk and packaged), the store was operated by volunteer workers and a manager who received a salary of $25 a week.

In August, 1970, the partnerships were dissolved and replaced by Earth Foods, Inc., a nonprofit corporation which assumed all assets and liabilities of the defunct partnerships. Concerts and other benefit activities sponsored by the organizations in Champaign and Urbana helped to raise $3000. In addition, a student organization at the University of Illinois donated $1000 to Earth Foods, Inc.

Decision-making is carried out by workers at weekly meetings which are open to all interested persons. Anyone is welcome to work in the store; they are paid, in merchandise, at an hourly rate. There are about twelve workers paid cash salaries, while some twenty others are paid in food. Their storefront is open seven days a week, from 9:00 A.M. to 9:00 P.M.

Essentially a food store, Earthworks sells dairy products and cheeses, organically grown produce, grains, seeds, beans, flour, loose and packaged herbs and spices, books, magazines, periodicals, handmade and factory-made pottery, Indian foods, a small selection of Amish-made clothes, some household items, and homemade products. Perhaps, with further expansion, Earthworks will handle frozen foods. The retail markup is between 20 to 25%.

There are some co-ops that seem to function as a center of activities in the community, and Earthworks is one of them. Since 1971, Earthworks has shared its building with a restaurant which serves "home-cooked meals." in August, 1970, Earthworks became involved with a preorder cooperative, which "has gone through several periods of waxing and waning and drifting away from the university community." Although independent of Earthworks, it has at times shared their building. In the following year, a group of individuals, many of whom had worked at Earthworks, set up another food store carrying a more traditional line of grocery items.

All these food operations share with Earthworks trucking services, the services of a bakery, and a heating, electrical, and refrigeration company—all started by people who at one time worked for Earthworks.

The building has provided sometimes inexpensive and often free space to the community, as well as to many enterprises—some of which have succeeded while others failed. Now sharing the building with Earthworks is the restaurant, a bike shop, and an electronic repairs shop.

YELLOW SUN NATURAL FOODS COOPERATIVE, INC.
35 North Pleasant Street
Amherst, Massachusetts 01002

This co-op, started in 1971, works out of a storefront open Monday through Saturday. There are four paid workers and 800 memberships. In order to join, members pay $20 a year per household of three and must put in three hours of work every other month. Since Amherst is a "farm-country and college-town community," there is a wide cross-section of members in terms of "occupation, temperament and crop involvement."

Demian, an assistant manager, explains the aims of the Yellow Sun Co-op: "Our jobs, as we see it, are first to get the best (cleanest, whole and natural) foods we can find for ourselves, friends and neighbors; and secondly, to educate ourselves and all others as to the role that food plays in the grand design of the universe."

The co-op sells produce, grains, dairy products, organic foods, hardware, and books. They carry about 2500 individual food, book, and hardware items.

Members pay a 5% markup over wholesale cost on most items. Nonmembers pay a 25% markup, which the Yellow Sun Co-op found to be lower on most items than other natural or specialty food stores in the Amherst area. Their "policy statement" explains that "the Yellow Sun is committed, at the lowest price we can find, to bring you the best, purest, most healthy food products that this planet offers." The co-op's policy further states that "as we are dedicated to being the most economical service to our members, we will sell to co-op members *anything* that they want in bulk—even if we do not recommend it. We will censor, however, what we sell to the general public, in accordance with what scientific information we can find."

There are many other buying clubs and storefront operations in Amherst. They have avoided some of the financial difficulties of the Yellow Sun Natural Foods Co-op by having a minimal overhead.

ANN ARBOR PEOPLE'S FOOD CO-OP
722 Packard
Ann Arbor, Michigan 48104

In the spring of 1971 this food co-op was started in a "small closet-like space" in the entrance to a local Ann Arbor head shop. At first this food store started out by selling honey, peanut butter, grains, home-baked rye bread, and mulberry pies. In time larger orders were organized with big co-ops, communes, and houses, and were operated by volunteer truckers and the store staff. At the present their inventory includes grains, organic foods (bread, baked goods, dried fruits), and dairy products. In the future they hope to sell organic fruit and vegetables grown by local farmers.

The Ann Arbor People's Food Co-op works out of a storefront open Monday through Saturday, 11:00 A.M. to 6:00 P.M., except on Wednesdays when the store is closed for cleaning. There are four paid workers. A second storefront is in the process of being set up. They are contemplating expanding into more neighborhood controlled local co-ops.

Their 3000 members include students, housewives, nurses, secretaries, laborers, and young people. Many of those who helped to start this food store had been politically active (SDS, White Panthers) prior to joining the co-op. Their basic aim is to provide food (specifically natural foods) at the lowest prices possible.

The Ann Arbor People's Food Co-op formerly supplied other co-ops, but found that this was too much to handle. Due to its large membership the co-op was able to help raise enough funds to establish a warehouse: The Michigan Federation of Food Co-ops Warehouse. The Ann Arbor group represents 50 to 60% of the warehouse's business, which also serves 20 to 30 other co-ops.

MILL CITY CO-OP
2552 Bloomington Avenue South
Minneapolis, Minnesota 55404

Mill City is run largely by volunteer help from the neighborhood and coordinated by six to eight workers who take the major responsibility. This offshoot of the North Country Co-op opened in January of 1972.

The "mother" store had become too busy to handle the entire load of the rapidly expanding cooperative community. Handbills were sent out in the fall of 1971 and a meeting was called to discuss the formation of a new co-op. From the seventy people who came, a handful volunteered their energies to bring the new storefront and equipment up to Health Department standards.

They tell of a series of difficulties that should be taken into account by anyone contemplating the formation of a store, or those operating an existing store.

Just about the time that Mill City was expanding and happily running in the black, they experienced a series of catastrophes: first a burglary of $300 worth of food stamps, a theft of $50 in cash, followed by the discovery that inexperienced volunteers at the cash registers and inaccurate scales were causing further losses.

The small markup of 10% was simply not enough to cover all these losses. However, at this point the neighborhood responded to the crisis by lending the store $2000.

By now, Mill City has learned the rhythms of food distribution, the potential areas of inefficiency, and the extent to which the honor system will work. They feel that Mill City Co-op has provided good food at low cost, and an experience in community cooperation.

OSHA FOOD CO-OP
8812 4th Street N.W.
Almeda, New Mexico 87114

This co-op started out in 1970 as a group of families buying together at wholesale prices. A year and a half later they moved to their present location—five acres with a storefront and eight families living on the land. The land used to be a junkyard, so the first year was spent clearing the land, planting, and remodelling the store.

They are presently negotiating to buy this land. If they succeed in doing so, they plan to farm most of the land and make Osha a community center for many different activities: setting up day care and craft centers, building greenhouses, and starting other co-ops.

At the moment all work is done on a voluntary basis. Those residing at Osha do not pay rent and they receive their food at cost. In exchange for these privileges, they accept the task of caretaking the land and store. Many members who do not live at Osha work for the store as cashiers, or making deliveries, cleaning, handling stock, and anything else that needs to be done. They are trying to encourage more outside members to participate in the responsibilities involved in the co-op's maintenance.

The Osha Food Co-op has about 1000 members; among them are students, businessmen, workers, professionals, and communes. There are general membership meetings held every six months when they elect a nine-member steering committee, which meets at least once a month. This group has the decision-making power for the co-op. One problem they are still faced with is trying to get enough people to do the necessary work. They may be forced to adopt work requirements starting in January, 1974.

FAMILY BUYING CLUB OF FLUSHING, INC.
202 Rocky Hill Road
Bayside, New York 11361

An unusual co-op formed in Flushing, New York, in 1968 with the simple requirement that the only members admitted were those families with four or more children. Their lawyer, who is also one of the original 30 members, said, "We felt that those who suffered the most from the inflation were the aged or large families. We decided that since we had similar needs, we could assemble our buying power and obtain the best savings from volume purchases."

By the time they had eighty families in 1969, they incorporated as the Family Buying Association, Inc., and moved into a 15 by 30 foot store. They grew slowly and carefully to keep costs down (their original store cost $90 a month).

One of the biggest difficulties was getting meat in quantities for a moderate cost. At one point they experimented with buying large roasts and bulk cuts from a restaurant supply house. They even tried to do their own meat cutting. Whatever method they used, it always ran into a loss for the co-op. Now that they are stabilized at 200 families and have moved into a larger store, they have hired a part-time butcher.

They have also had the usual difficulties with volunteer help and found that by hiring one of their more active members as a permanent manager they have better stability. She is supplemented by a volunteer staff that donates three hours of work every six weeks.

While the original founders were mostly lawyers and accountants, the larger proportion of their members are now blue-collar workers.

They no longer have the large family requirement for membership.

They purchase their staples from Mid-Eastern Cooperative, the same supplier that serves the cooperative supermarkets with the Twin Pine emblems on the Northeast coast. Through membership in a wholesale cooperative, they are able to buy their staples from among the 6000 items that Mideastern stocks. In turn, they have a representative on the board of the wholesale cooperative.

With a sense of cooperation, good organization, and management, they have used their combined $450,000 a year food bill to stretch their buying power. The Association's members have adapted to shopping a few days a week, added a little of their own labor, and found an alternative to supermarket prices.

NORTH BUFFALO COMMUNITY FOOD CO-OP
3225 Main Street
Buffalo, New York 14214

Inspired by the Lexington Avenue Co-op in Buffalo, people connected with the State University of New York at Buffalo were able to get an appropriation from the student association of the University to form a co-op. Out of $5400 which was appropriated, about $3000 was used to set up the North Buffalo Community Food Co-op. It was begun in September, 1971, and opened for business in February, 1972, and since then has operated successfully.

The North Buffalo Co-op works out of an off-campus storefront open Monday through Saturday, 10:00 A.M. to 6:00 P.M., Thursdays until 8:00 P.M. Except for its three paid coordinators at $30 a week, the store staff is made up of volunteers. The co-op has a total membership of 300; about 50% are students. It sells produce, grains, dairy products, and organic foods at a 30 to 40% markup, with a 14.3% discount for members.

The North Buffalo Co-op has an additional feature in its storefront: a free store. People bring in whatever usable items (mostly clothes and books) they no longer need, and are able to take home, at no charge, anything they find they can use.

Jim Stumm, one of the co-ordinators, expresses his mixed feelings about the co-op: "Our larger purpose is to develop a sense of community and to help people to provide for other needs besides food, although little has been visibly accomplished in this direction. We are very successful at providing good food at low prices, however, and sometimes I suspect we have done more at forming a community than appears at first glance. Some days I feel very strongly that a co-op community does exist here. However we have a long way to go.''

ORGANIC ENERGY CO-OP
68-06 Fresh Meadow Lane
Flushing, New York 11365

It is organic food, of course, for the six hundred members that make up the largest co-op of its kind in Queens. There is a constant check on their suppliers to verify the ''natural'' aspect of the food.

During a visit to a plant, one of the members found that rennet was being added to the cheese, and a better source was located. Since much of the food is higher than supermarket prices, vigilance is necessary.

The co-op divides the managerial duties among three paid workers. Since its inception in 1970, begun by some Queens College students, they have come a long way in operational efficiency.

The store is simple but clean, with produce sold directly from the crates. At one time a class in Yoga, held in the back of the store, helped to create an offshoot to the food operation. About ten members formed a house commune and a nearby natural-food restaurant. Many members eat there and volunteer their help as well.

A portion of the membership comes from the local middle-class community. This is a further indication that people are willing to pay and work for food which they hope is not doused with sprays and loaded with preservatives.

In addition to produce and dairy products, Organic Energy also supplies the usual grains, nuts, etcetera. The combined volume is between $600 and $800 a day.

Despite the hope for a more perfect community, many co-ops face the problem of pilferage by members as well as the general public. This is more apparent in the big-city environment. At any rate some people that are otherwise honest, irrationally seem to feel that they are still entitled to free food and books, even though they are no longer children.

All food stores have this problem, and big-city supermarkets most of all. Donna, one of the members, said: "It is very difficult. Some of these people are your friends. The managers have to speak to them and it's not pleasant."

Organic Energy has found that they have to be tighter in all their operations as time goes by. With 600 members, they now require that everyone present their membership card at the cash register.

This does not alter the friendly atmosphere, it just helps to keep them "in the black." Members pay $5 a year dues, 10% markup and contribute two hours of work per month. Nonmembers pay 20% above cost price.

Future plans for Organic Energy include their own direct source of produce, perhaps even their own farm. Meanwhile, they get direct shipments of carloads of produce from an organic/natural farmer in California.

THE BROADWAY LOCAL FOOD CO-OP (CONSPIRACY)
718 Columbus Avenue
New York, New York 10025

The Broadway Local Food Co-op (or Conspiracy) is a food-buying club and was started by three Bronx High School of Science students as a social science project, early in 1971. They found an abandoned city-owned building and used the storefront as headquarters for a co-op based on a Cambridge, Massachusetts, model. Since they have no mailing facilities or telephone, you must go to the storefront for information about membership.

The response was so enthusiastic that the thirty or forty families quickly had to reorganize. The early chaos was controlled by forming "bloc" groups, or small local buying clubs, that sent representatives to pick up food and help distribute from the storefront.

They are a little cramped by their 13 x 50 foot storefront but the price is right: $1 a year rent to the city. The two hundred and fifty members spread from the Lincoln Center area to the 180's.

The membership is as diverse and lively as the West Side of Manhattan itself, but, as Natalie Silverstein says, "We don't have as many disadvantaged people as we had hoped for. We all thought that this would bring the neighborhood together. (There are luxury buildings as well as subsidized housing in the immediate vicinity.) But the people don't understand buying for something on Monday and not getting it until Friday. They don't trust this."

There are other problems when a middle-class venture tries to reach people with other lifestyles. "The men feel that this is woman's work and the women are too busy."

Broadway Local hammered out each step of their way: discussing, making lists, order forms, buying sheets, and finding information. Finally they started with produce, grains, and bread. Then they added eleven dairy items, and after a few months, meat. Every decision evolved out of Wednesday night discussions.

They have their own reconditioned mail truck for produce bought at the Hunts Point Market. The bread and meat are delivered to the storefront. Yogurt and some other items are supplied by a local grocer at a slight markup.

All food is sold at a 5% markup. But some members are concerned that the extra food is sold to people without extra cost or effort on their part. As in any other group activity, there are members who tend to accept the responsibilities and the heavy work while others are content to keep involvement to a minimum. Eventually the "heavies" start making the decisions as well.

The Broadway Local has made strong attempts to keep the group democratic. This is an excerpt from their bulletin:

> Some co-op members think they are alienated from the decision-making process in the co-op, and indeed this is true. In order to become involved in the decision-making process you first of all must attend Wednesday night meetings, and secondly volunteer to do some of the work that is done by the Wednesday night heavies. For example, people are needed to:
>
> 1 Deal with the Agricultural Department, Health Department, Insurance, Urban Renewal (lease and repairs), Con Ed.

2 Organize storefront repairs, check daily to see that the store has not been broken into.
3 Look around for butchers, new items (coffee and sharp cheddar).
4 Keep track of the bank account, write out checks, stamp and deposit all food coupons.

These are a few of the things that were done or are being done by 'Wednesday night heavies.' They do it because no one else will do it. In reality, the Wednesday night heavies are probably the most cooperative group in the co-op; the problem is that there is no one to cooperate with.

Despite the occasional difficulties, which arise in the best-run groups, the typical atmosphere at the store is cheerful and busy.

The food was selling for one-third or one-half less than the supermarket price and the volunteers were efficiently packaging "bloc" orders. Others came to call for their orders, and the goodwill and camaraderie were a pleasant change from the plastic or indifferent supermarket.

THE GREENHOUSE ASSOCIATION
466 Amsterdam Avenue
New York, New York 10024

The largest natural/organic food co-op in New York, started in early 1970, to combat the high markup in health food stores. In that short time they have acquired 1400 members and now have a volume of $37,000 a month.

This sort of natural food co-op appeals to many busy New Yorkers with its professionally run, efficient store. Their full-time manager, Gus, mans a tight ship and cuts down on the problematical nature of many co-op food store operations.

Even though members contribute four hours of work every quarter, there is some "flak" from the larger cooperative community. There are some that are opposed, on principle, to a co-op manager receiving the prevailing community wages. Despite the professionalism, a clublike atmosphere exists in the busy store.

The large membership prefers this type of organization. It enables them to engage in other activities while still maintaining a cooperative base. They feel that there is enough room for variations to suit the needs of individual groups.

Greenhouse carries produce, meat, groceries, canned goods, and fifty-seven varieties of cheese as well as the usual "health" type foods. The beef is raised for them by Paul Moore in Pennsylvania. The grains come from the Village Market in New York as well as other natural/organic distributors.

This nonprofit co-op, which is open Tuesday through Saturday, holds two meetings a year. The markup ranges from 20 to 25% which Gus claims is "still about 33 to 45% lower than the health food stores."

THE WILD RICE ORGANIC FOOD CO-OP
325 West 16th Street
New York, New York 10011

On the second floor of an old loft building in the Chelsea area, is a clean, cheerful, and well-run natural food co-op. There are attractive samples of all the food Wild Rice stocks in a cozy sitting area. Members can browse through a magazine, chat with friends, or quickly get down to business and mark their order sheets.

Each of the three volunteer managers that have worked in the co-op since 1970 has brought new innovations to meet changing needs. Wild Rice has learned from previous errors and now has a soundly run co-op.

One summer during this period, one of the most active workers lived and ate at the co-op. Wild Rice found that in addition to other small "leaks," the cost of his food wiped out their surplus completely.

The previous manager had brought some excellent business practices that proved to be too costly for a marginally run operation. The printed business forms and paper bags had to be eliminated.

Everyone predicted that the co-op would fail, but emergency methods in addition to the membership deposits pulled them through. These are some of the measures taken:

1 They moved to a cheaper location across the hall and reduced the rent to $160 a month.
2 The phone bill was cut to one quarter of the previous amount. (No unnecessary calls were allowed by members. The Pennsylvania produce supplier accepted their order calls collect because their account was always up to date.)
3 They stopped buying bags and wrapping material. By charging five cents for a small paper bag, members got the message and brought their own bags and jars.
4 The co-op members brought the empty cartons to a recycling center and saved carting expenses. (The co-op supermarket in the Brentwood section of L.A. is among one of the many co-ops that run a recycling center.)
5 The manager did a little investigating and found the proper person to give permission for free garbage removal. (As a nonprofit organization they are entitled to this service.)
6 The most dramatic change was the switch to volunteer workers prepackaging loose products.

The last change was reluctantly voted for after two weeks of controlled experiments. The Wild Rice Co-op membership discovered that the open bins of raisins and nuts were too tempting. Some members were taking a handful to munch as they did their shopping. One was simply loading up his car and paying $5. Others were just a little over on the scale. It was all adding up to insolvency.

They were disappointed, but faced the necessity to keep the food supplies separate from the shoppers. The Wild Rice membership decided that it was a big-city phenomenon that they could not change.

Despite the loss of the country store atmosphere, Ron Short reports: "There is a sense of family because the members enjoy working together despite their differences."

And they are *all* different: doctors, lawyers, vegetarians, accountants, Orthodox Jews and Moslems, feminists, and macrobiotics followers, some elderly, some young. Despite the fact that they have varied lifestyles and sometimes belong to factions that think differently, they all have something in common—they are turning away from supermarkets and TV dinners.

They once voted on whether or not to maintain the volunteer system or get a paid manager. It was decided that, "If people did not work, it would simply be a cheap A & P and that is not what we want." (The volunteer time is six hours per quarter.)

But it is cheap, considerably cheaper, even the meat. And it works.

CAPITOL HILL CO-OP
1835 12th Avenue
Seattle, Washington 98122

This food store was organized in 1971 by eight individuals who provided capital for the original investment and have since been reimbursed through the co-op's profits over a period of time. The Capitol Hill Co-op works out of a storefront and is open six days a week, seven hours a day. Two of its workers are paid a subsistence allowance. There are 190 members, each of whom must contribute five hours of work per month. The markup is 15% for members, while it is 1% for cashiers and managers who must work a minimum of five hours each week; nonmembers pay a 30% markup. The Capitol Hill Co-op sells grains, produce, dairy products, and organic foods. Among their wholesalers is the Cooperating Community.

WHOLE EARTH LEARNING COMMUNITY
817 East Johnson Street
Madison, Wisconsin 53703

One of the more active health food groups that started in 1969 as the Whole Earth Co-op, this co-op is typical of the groups who are using the co-op concept as a path to a better life. They have a cheerful store that stocks much of the usual health foods, books, and utensils, but they try to buy as much of the merchandise as possible from local suppliers, partially to support people in their own area and decentralize food merchandizing to achieve a self-sufficient community.

Organized in 1969 as a storefront co-op, the people who started Whole Earth were "interested in radically changing their lifestyles and wanted to have access to the information and the material they needed to actually do it. They wanted to live more in harmony with the natural world, to simplify their daily lives and to escape the 9 to 5 crush of the city" (Dedaimia Krejci from *The Learning Net*, Winter, 1972).

In 1971, the Whole Earth Co-op, as it was then called, changed its name to the Whole Earth Learning Community. At that time its legal structure also underwent a change from a co-op to a nonprofit corporation of the educational variety.

Since then, classes have been set up; they offer instruction in cooking, canning, weaving, embroidery, nutrition, foraging for plants, religion, math, winemaking, piano, and guitar. A newsletter, *The Learning Net*, was also started with the idea of "putting people in touch with those who could teach them what they wanted to learn."

Whole Earth works out of a storefront open every day except Wednesday, from noon to 9:00 P.M. It is run by a group of some fifteen to twenty-five volunteers, in addition to a staff of five paid workers who receive a subsistence salary. In the spring of 1971, it was decided that this paid staff would rotate every six months in order to "make it possible for more people to become involved in the store at the heart of things and to actually acquire the skills needed to keep the Whole Earth together."

Among their members are many university students as well as neighborhood students, older people, and middle-aged, middle-class people interested in natural foods. They sell grains, produce, dairy products, organic foods (although almost everything they sell is organic), nuts and seeds, dried fruit, herbs and spices, books and tools. They have a 30% markup on all items.

Between four and five every afternoon is the Quiet Hour, when the store is not open for business. "This hour is for people who want to come in, sip tea, read or talk to one another."

Whole Earth Learning Community is part of a larger group of organizations with similar philosophies. Among such organizations are "Nature's Bakery," "Common Market," and "Mifflin Street."

CAMPUS CO-OPS

Many co-ops originated on campuses within the available building space with students eager for new group efforts. Some also had the preliminary funding from the school itself. Others have grown out of the common need for inexpensive food in cooperative student housing. One of the original food co-ops started at Berkeley in the 1930's. Many leaders and organizers of co-ops today had first been involved in student co-ops while they were at school.

Due to the transient nature of a college community, one problem which many campus co-ops are faced with is a lack of permanence and stability in their internal organization. For example, a co-op was started at Brown University in Providence, Rhode Island, but was forced to close down due to a lack of student interest or involvement.

But many university-based co-ops have grown and survived. One of the largest of these is the Boston Food Co-op, which started out in the fall of 1971 as a campus buying club with a membership of some 100 families. It worked out of the Boston University student union selling fresh produce. By the end of 1972 the co-op had moved to a small factory building not far from the University campus.

Membership is $3 per member of a household; in addition each member must volunteer a minimum of two hours per month which may involve putting away food, working the cash register, or picking up food from suppliers. The Boston Food Co-op has somewhere between five and six thousand members, 2000 of whom are active. Many of the co-op's members are students and young working people. The Boston Co-op is also trying to reach other members in the community such as the poor and the retired. The co-op is open to nonmembers as well.

The co-op now carries a wide line of produce, dairy products, grains, meats, canned goods, and household supplies. The prices that are carefully checked run 15 to 20% below prices charged by supermarkets in the area.

This change in the co-op's policy was facilitated by freezers and coolers (either purchased secondhand or supplied by wholesalers) which enabled them to store perishables. With a somewhat larger inventory, they were able to absorb any fluctuations in demand.

Since the co-op's membership is so extensive, sudden changes in buying patterns tend to average out.

The Boston Co-op has helped other New England co-ops in getting started; it also founded the federation, NEFCO. They publish their own newsletter and have plans to build a playground area outside the store for young children while their parents shop in the co-op.

In his article "The Boston Co-op," published in the *Journal of the New Harbinger*, Matthew Perlson writes about the co-op's policy on its food inventory: "Unlike many other food co-ops we have not limited our inventory to exclude foods which are considered uneconomical or unnutritious. Instead, what we carry is stocked in response to requests from the membership.

"We feel that where there is lack of agreement, limiting of the items available results in either forcing certain segments of our community out of the co-op, or imposing the will of one segment on another—contrary to the principles of economic democracy. To compensate for unhealthy consumption habits, we provide the membership with the maximum amount of information available on food buying and nutrition."

chapter 5

The Cooperative Supermarket

The scope of this book does not permit a detailed analysis of how to set up a large cooperative supermarket. However, much can be learned from examining the method of operation and what they offer before making a choice for yourself.

Many of the large cooperative supermarkets that look as if they have sprung full-grown into the established marketplace, started 40 years ago in a form similar to the food-buying clubs and food conspiracies now springing up across the country. Some started as community efforts by dedicated people who sought an alternative way of distribution in an economy that did not seem to work.

During the Depression of the thirties, farmers went broke with crops that no one could afford to buy while the unemployed stood in bread lines begging for food. Recent college graduates, union members, ministers, and professors experimented with buying clubs as a means of self-help. Many were newly poor, others social visionaries. Working together they revitalized the consumer co-op movement in the United States.

In New York City, a food co-op was started in a basement of one of the Bronx Amalgamated Cooperative houses in 1930 and grossed $100 a day. In the mid-thirties four families organized a consumers' club in Ithaca, New York, and rented a stall in a local farmers' market and opened three days a week. There was hope of doing away with the profit motive and "wasteful and unpleasant competition," and the early cooperators spoke of "the new fellowship of cooperation."*

By the late thirties and early forties the clubs expanded to the extent

*An Adventure in Cooperation, by Hugh Cosline, New York, Arnold Printing Co.

that they could open small stores. Many members helped finance
their investments through credit unions, another form of cooperative.
The extensive Finnish population in Berkeley and Fort Bragg had a
well-established cooperative tradition and joined with the chain of
cooperatives that were growing in California.

The cooperatives that survived the severe competition of the post-
war period and the advent of easier money and shiny new supermarkets had something else to offer. They too, became supermarkets
with efficient management, record keeping and sound funding. They
needed constant communication with their members to maintain
consumer loyalty through special services and information. Many
succeeded in maintaining the delicate balance between idealism and
practical economics.

Most of the co-op food stores that have survived into the difficult
food market of the seventies have either been based in middle-class
communities, located in cooperative houses, perhaps having the
support of a socially aware movement, or a cohesive labor group as in
Akron, Ohio.

Whether or not the members know about the original Rochdale
experiment in early eighteenth-century England, it is founded on
these principles:

1 Open membership.
2 One member, one vote.
3 Limited or no interest on investment shares.
4 Savings or profits distributed to members.

They pay the same rate of taxes as other stores, but the money
returned at the end of the year to a member-consumer is considered to
be a refund and is not taxed. Sometimes as much as half of the sales
slips are not turned in and this money is subject to federal and local
taxes. The balance is added to a small percentage of the profit to form
a cash reserve. They effect the same savings as a well-run supermarket by joining together with other cooperative markets and perhaps
pharmacies, optical centers, furniture, television and radio service
centers into a federation of cooperatives. Several of these federations are in turn able to support and obtain supplies at regional warehouse centers established across the country. Presumably, this

enables the individual stores to make the same bulk savings as large food chains. However, the San Francisco Bay area is one of the few places in which they have become a major competitor.

Is the food cheaper in a cooperative supermarket? Not substantially, but their house brands which are quality controlled and graded are cheaper than the national name brand, and some stores consistently give patronage refunds. If your need is to make a substantial savings on your weekly grocery bill, this form of cooperative buying is not for you.

It is estimated that 60 to 65% of the average food bill is overhead and labor. Most supermarkets run on an 18 to 20% markup. Since this form of market is run exclusively with paid employees, the profit margin is the same as the average chain, which is between 1 and 3% in good years. Incredible? Well, the total sales of the large chains runs into billions of dollars each year and a profit margin of 1 or 2% is substantial. It also explains why the Mom and Pop stores cannot keep afloat with competitive prices.

If a family spends $40 a week in the cooperative supermarket and the profit at the end of the year is 1-1/2%, then the savings would be thirty dollars, which is the equivalent of three-fourths of a week's groceries free. A membership share in a co-op supermarket ranges from $25 in the older societies to $50 in the newer supermarkets. Most have a system of "eat your way into membership." At the end of a year, a patron can take 20% of the refund on purchases in cash and the remaining 80% will apply toward a share of stock. Without a cash outlay, a customer can become a member and have a share that can be redeemed for cash.

The patron is the owner of the store and that essentially accounts for the existence of the cooperative more often than the moderate savings. While the manager is under some pressure to insure savings, the policies, pricing, type of food, cleanliness, and services are determined by the members.

While endless debate occurred in New York City between the Office of Consumer Affairs and the supermarket chains on the feasibility of unit pricing, the local cooperative stores simply proceeded to put it into effect. The other chains were forced to follow. Similarly, the existence of a co-op frequently forces a neighborhood store to drop its prices.

The management of the stores depends on feedback from the members to inform them of the changes and services expected. The average co-op member can expect not to be cheated by unfair advertising and merchandising practices. Through extensive consumer education, and membership with other consumer groups can be a pressure for consumer protection legislation.

Seymour Klanfer of the New York Federation of Cooperatives is proud of the quality of the foods carried in the eleven member co-op stores. He speaks with pride about the quality of the meat and the control exercised. "We are one of the very few meat buyers in the city of New York who still have the privilege of going into the rail cars to put our own identification stamp on sides of beef . . . we have been in business for over forty years and we have established a relationship . . ."

They keep full-time meat, grocery, and produce buyers. The latter starts at three or four in the morning, walking the miles of Hunts Point market, checking on store needs by telephone and buying produce as needed. There is also a grocery and meat supervisor to check on display and freshness. Unlike many supermarkets which are cutting their costs, only U.S. choice meat is sold and it is grade one. (There are five qualities of grade choice.)

It all seems to pay off. The appearance of the stores and the food rate high in a city often noted for its indifferent markets in marginal areas. They have fewer sanitary violations, and the U.S.D.A. inspector who is asked to make surprise visits frequently, reports all food to be of top quality.

Sometimes all that care is not enough to survive in a time when there is a price war going on in food chain store operations. Many patrons are lured away by discount prices on some items and some stores that have gone into big expansive programs are showing no profits. The operation of food supermarkets has been hazardous for commercial chains and cooperatives alike. One chain has been reported to have lost fifty million dollars in the first eight months of 1972. It may be time to rethink the entire supermarket concept if our economy does not stabilize.

According to *Supermarket News*, the top ten chain stores averaged 0.24% margin in 1972 and the largest forty-eight chains suffered a

75.8% drop in profit. It seems extremely risky for any group to establish a new supermarket today (even with all the essentials), the chances of failure are high at the present in any competitive area.

Most of the large cooperative supermarkets have the Twin Pine emblem on their storefront indicating that they are affiliated with the Cooperative League of the U.S.A. This organization consists of consumer goods and food co-ops, credit unions, farm credit systems, farm, fishing, electric and insurance co-ops, and many others with a total of 24 million members.

There has been some discussion in recent years as to whether or not the League is aimed at helping the consumer co-ops, with less than a half million members, or favors the well-established and government-aided farmers and dairy co-ops. They have been trying to steer a middle course to serve all their members. The forward-looking California consumers' cooperatives has joined the League. They, as well as others in the organization, may activate the development of an urban credit system for co-ops, as well as fight for more helpful legislation. It has been suggested that without some government help such as the farm co-ops received in the twenties, consumer co-ops will always have a struggle to exist.

If you are thinking of forming your own store, the Cooperative League of the U.S.A., at 1828 L Street N.W., Washington, D.C., 20036, has developed extensive manuals of organization and record-keeping as well as films. This project should only be attempted if there is not a co-op supermarket nearby, or if there are poor shopping facilities. The League is funded by government contract to aid the formation of cooperatives in underdeveloped countries, but does not itself have the manpower or funds to help groups here.

Since it takes two or three years to set up a supermarket of this sort, a contract has to be made with an organizer. If you have a serious group or a storefront operation that would like to move on, contact them for a list. So far they have been more successful with middle-class groups than those in low-income areas. At present they are at work with an organizer in a badly decaying section of Brooklyn that is the focus of a large urban revitalization program. If it succeeds, it will be one of the few to work in a purely low-income setting.

To sum up, one joins a cooperative supermarket if:

1 It is reasonably convenient.
2 You have neither the time or inclination to be more involved with a smaller group.
3 You are willing to save money by using co-op brands.
4 Your shopping habits require one-stop shopping.
5 You want the assurance that you are not being cheated by unfair promotion.
6 You prefer the stability that comes with a professionally managed store.
7 You want consumer protection.

chapter 6

The New Cooperative Warehouses and Federations

The natural outgrowth of the new form of cooperative food store is a federation. This is meant to put together both the source of the food (small farmers, crafts people, or mills) and the individual co-ops.

Warehouses have existed for years in a different form, founded by the older, more established co-ops that are members of the League of Cooperatives of the U.S.A. They have several regional warehouses across the country that stock about 6000 items each.

These organizations are not completely satisfactory answers for the many new styles of co-ops that have developed in the past decade. This is partially because they require investment in the existing cooperative warehouse, and partially because they stock items that the new co-ops are not interested in—some empty-calorie foods and processed items.

Only in the California region, where a progressive cooperative operation has been established for more than thirty years and where the co-ops have a large share of the total market, is there a facility that stocks the type of food and shares the philosophy of part of the new movement.

While the large regional warehouses have been excellent sources for the co-op supermarkets, the new co-ops seek a small warehouse operation more tailored to a new way of life.

Each area has a slightly different type of operation, mostly influenced by the needs of the community, the funds available, and the personal style of the most active organizers and workers.

Some are still in the early stages of development, and will change as they grow to suit the needs and involvement of the community. One thing is certain, where there is a good warehouse operation, the small co-ops thrive.

Some co-op stores which have available space also serve as a center for buying groups and smaller co-ops in a convenient area. There is sometimes a blurred edge between a storefront depot and a warehouse.

The policy decisions for the federation are generally established by the managers of the individual co-op stores or large buying groups, and sometimes by representatives from the producers (farmers, etcetera).

The most active men and women of the co-ops have been seeking a better and alternative way of doing the necessary business of life in a more human and less competitive way. Yet the running of a federation can be a jolting experience.

Most of the managers of the new co-ops, and some farmers as well, are highly educated and articulate people. They also have a sense of the rightness of conducting a federation in a particular way. It is also clear to an observer that this kind of organization and management skill, placed in the business world, would earn a sizable amount of money.

The necessity of rules and methods are even more apparent in an organization that serves so many different co-ops. Many of the representatives have been working hard and effectively in groups and have evolved their own philosophies.

Some have chosen not to join a federation because of the loss of autonomy by the individual store or buying group. Others have found that the federation does not change their operation to any noticeable degree and is a most effective solution to cutting costs.

Still other individuals have complained of the pettiness, self-righteousness, lack of organization, and lack of discipline they have found in the formation of a federation. Despite all this, some have managed to work out a compromise and push the project forward.

The following is a survey of a few large operations which are still growing. They welcome inquiries and some also advise co-ops on methods.

CORNUCOPIA
2808 West Lake Street
Chicago, Illinois 60612

One of the largest federations of food cooperatives is located on the West Side of Chicago. It is well situated to serve one of the poorest areas of the city—and still available to the rest of the Chicago area.

Opened in March, 1972, it serves some 4500 member families in a 16,000-square-foot warehouse. With ten workers paid at prevailing wages, they manage a volume of $7000 weekly, at a considerable saving to their patrons.

Their motto is "Food For All The People—Together." They consider that "food at prices everyone can afford is a basic human right. But the only way that people have been able to secure their rights is by joining together—by organizing."

Despite the fact that Chicago is one of the important food distribution points, many low-income families have found themselves trapped by rising food costs. Through the proliferation of buying clubs and small food co-ops during 1969-70 there has been some success in reaching the people most affected by spreading poverty. In many areas the concept of planning, ordering, and paying in advance has been a major block in reaching those who most desperately need good food at reasonable prices.

Several diverse programs have helped organize these clubs among people who usually do not have enough money to pay in advance for groceries (or in fact for anything). By 1971 the need to coordinate their diffuse efforts to achieve savings became apparent. There was no previously existing warehouse that was tailored for their needs. And their orientation literature tells how "a small group of people deeply committed to the co-op movement came together to consider alternatives. The members of this original task force felt that to reach more low-income families, a well-run warehouse facility designed specifically to serve them, was essential."

Funding was received from the Cook County Office of Economic Opportunity, The Willbolt Foundation, the American Freedom From Hunger Foundation, and the W. Clement and Jessie V. Stone Foundation. The operations are based on the assumption that

Cornucopia is now an independent, self-sufficient, cooperatively run warehouse.

The markup of the wholesale costs averages between 18-1/2 and 20%. Less stable items are marked up more than nonperishables. The resulting margin serves to pay all operation costs and the markup is reduced as the volume increases.

The savings are largest on produce and some organic/natural foods. One of the workers, Claudia, says: "Our grain and meat prices are not a great deal cheaper than store prices but we feel our quality is *much* better."

In addition to meat, produce, and grains they carry an extensive list of dairy products, provisions, dried fruits, and nuts. The poor quality of food, especially meat, in low-income areas is notorious. With the gradual abandonment of supermarkets in many inner-city areas, the co-op fills an essential need.

It has been the focal point of an important self-help program. Through seminars, neighborhood meetings, a weekly bulletin, and other literature, members are informed about nutrition, economical buying, and consumer issues, as well as ways to solve the problems that arise in any cooperative group. As in any other cooperative ventures (or perhaps any business or organization), Cornucopia reports, ". . . ups and downs that would fill a good-sized book. But despite the hard lessons, the problems and disagreements, and the occasional threat of financial disaster, Cornucopia has continued to serve the people—and thousands of them are able to feed their families better, at significantly lower cost, because it exists."

There is no membership fee at Cornucopia. The only prerequisite for joining is a refundable deposit, approximately the amount of the buying club's weekly order. The deposit is kept in a special buying fund used exclusively to make purchases of food ordered by the co-op. A special arrangement is made for groups that cannot afford the deposit. No new co-op members are turned away because they cannot afford the deposit. Complete order forms and plainly written instructions on how a buying club works are given to the group.

Clubs vary from 3 to 4 families to larger groups and extend to the surrounding suburbs. There is also a 10 to 15% student membership. Some of the grains are obtained through cooperating federations in

Minneapolis and in Madison, Wisconsin, as well as from local sources. Most of the produce comes from the South Water markets but there is a search on for some direct farm sources.

GLUT
4005 34th Street
Mt. Rainier, Maryland 20812

Started in 1969, Glut is a warehouse operation which services over 1000 members in some 60 co-ops and buying clubs throughout the Washington, D.C., Virginia, and Maryland area. Its membership consists of young, "alternate-lifestyle" people (about 50%), conservative businessmen, professionals, and housewives—all working together.

Glut works out of a warehouse which is in fact a storefront along the lines of an old-fashioned grocery store. Ten part-time workers paid subsistence salaries help to keep the co-op open Wednesday through Sunday. The store is open to the public on Saturday and Sunday to sell surplus foods. There are shelves lined with canned goods, barrels of grain in the center, and at the back of the store is a refrigerated case for meat and cheese.

Biggest savings are on fresh produce; Glut's prices in this category are often half what supermarkets charge. The savings on meat and cheese are substantial, but on much of the canned goods, the supermarket offers lower prices than Glut.

Cattle are raised by local farmers for Glut and are taken to a butcher in Germantown, Pennsylvania, for slaughter. These cows have been raised in as chemical-free an environment as possible. The beef is natural, and it is "US Good" quality. There is a debate going on in the co-op at the moment as to whether or not they should sell Black Angus beef, which would result in a higher grade but would cost about 4¢ more per pound.

The debate of cost versus moral issues has plagued Glut as well as many other co-ops. Decisions of this sort are worked out at meetings.

In the past, Glut was faced with the problem of not being able to offer its members enough savings compared with supermarket prices.

Many people left the co-op and Glut soon had a major crisis on its hands. They gained ideas from experienced cooperators which helped them to operate more efficiently.

This crucial battle having been won, Glut stands on solid ground as a depot-warehouse operation which is able to offer people quality food at considerable savings in an atmosphere of friendliness and honesty. Although Glut does not call itself a federation by name, it basically functions as one.

NEW ENGLAND FOOD COOPERATING ORGANIZATION
(NEFCO) (operating out of the Boston Food Co-op)
12-14 Babbitt Street
Boston, Massachusetts 02215

When Roger Auerbach took over the management of the Boston Food Co-op in January, 1973, he was well aware of the need for a wholesale buying operation. His previous experience had been with the large Mission Hill buying club in the Boston vicinity. (In the morning, before he left for his job as a lawyer with the Housing and Urban Development Organization in Boston, he did some of their main food purchasing.)

NEFCO was started the previous September by the Boston Co-op to meet the needs of the fifteen small local co-ops. Roger said, ''The small clubs just can't survive without getting case prices on produce and other items. They lose their members if they are not able to buy in quantity.''

Brokerage was the original activity, according to their announcement. By buying together NEFCO members are able to deal with the wholesalers who receive the whole carload of produce, cutting out the secondary wholesaler who also buys from that primary receiver. Quality goes up and price goes down. This service is available to large and small co-ops for 10¢ a case or half-case. Co-ops interested in this aspect of NEFCO should write or call Roger Auerbach, c/o Boston Food Co-op, 12-14 Babbitt Street, Boston, Massachusetts 02215 (Phone: 617-267-9090).

The function of NEFCO at this time is to supply the seven or eight local co-ops directly out of the co-op while the remainder arrange for delivery. Much of the produce comes from the local wholesale market but they have a ''back to the farm'' plan: NEFCO will try to deal as much as possible with local farmers who grow wholesome food and want to sell it at equitable prices. Also, they will be working on the possibilities of buying grains and nuts and other goodies direct from their suppliers all over the country.

But their overall objective is larger in scope. NEFCO is planning to be a source of educational materials on foods and co-op management as well.

In discussing the structure of the new co-ops, Roger Auerbach said, ''There is a fear of the bureaucracy that comes out of formal management policies. But somehow there has to be in order to be a structure that will allow for more efficient operations in some of the co-ops.''

The long-term plan is to organize the community enough to set up a cooperative construction group. There are enough people available with the technical skills to gut and rehabilitate some of the substandard local buildings. (This has been successfully accomplished by a food cooperative in Harlem. See Chapter 8 on Low-Income Co-ops.)

Other plans are also being developed elsewhere in the NEFCO group. Don Lubin and Nancy Jean Barbier, two of the active members of the Free Venice Co-op, are among those trying to form a larger organization with wide participation.

The structure will be as follows: NEFCO will be incorporated in Massachusetts as a nonprofit corporation. Its members will be food cooperatives. Its decision-making body will be a board of directors, consisting of one representative from each member. Each director will have an equal vote. Because of the wide geographic area covered by NEFCO, they foresee many of its activities being carried on regionally.

THE MICHIGAN FEDERATION OF FOOD CO-OPS
(a mill and a wherehouse)
404 West Huron Street
Ann Arbor, Michigan 48103

The warehouse idea grew as the many co-ops in and around Ann Arbor began to see that joint buying would be mutually beneficial. Sheryl Green, a former member, describes the process:

"People began to meet every two weeks with representatives from all the food-related co-ops in Michigan (including food co-ops, farming co-ops, and bakery co-ops). After considerable discussion they came up with by-laws, a corporation, a mill, and a warehouse."

When the Ann Arbor co-op found that they had too much business to handle themselves, they became active in raising the original investment for the Federation. At this point they account for 50 to 60% of the purchases, while the other twenty-five to thirty co-ops account for the remainder of the $16,000 monthly volume.

Since 1972, when the Federation was founded, they have added to their size and inventory regularly. They now sell grains, beans, and cheese at a 10 percent markup. Sheryl describes some of the other efforts of the various local co-ops. "Food people tried to bake bread to fill orders through the co-op. After many attempts to use the ovens of the large housing co-ops, it was decided to rent bakery facilities for a night or two. Today the bakery operates full-time."

In the fall apples are picked by food co-op people and both apples and apple cider are offered through the co-op. In Michigan, the warehouse idea is an idea whose time has come.

NORTH COUNTRY COOPERATIVE PEOPLE'S WAREHOUSE
2129 Riverside
Minneapolis, Minnesota 55415

It is probably not accidental that the largest and strongest of the new cooperative federations are in the Midwest, formerly the center of the farmer-labor alliance and populist movement of the late nineteenth and early twentieth centuries.

The participants these days are frequently college-trained workers, farmers and young professional people, but the same trend exists to form new alliances for strength in the face of big business power.

One of the large new federations started in Minneapolis-St. Paul and found a home in a country-type co-op. The style of the new movement people would astonish their grandfathers and great-grandfathers. The cheery informal conferences are complete with rap sessions. Various forms of co-ops in the area, as well as those from afar, met in the fall of 1973.

Completely serious workshop sessions were held to work out details of interstate trucking, warehousing, co-op politics, and the sharing of resources and energy. This follows the same pattern for federations previously developed in Wisconsin and Michigan.

The center for all this and the federation as well is the North Country Co-op. The following report on the Co-op was drawn from a piece in the magazine *Lifestyle!* by Lynda McDonnell.

> If the spirit is strong, a co-op can begin anywhere—even on a back porch of someone's home. That's where the North Country Co-op of Minneapolis began: selling whole wheat flour, brown rice, oatmeal, and honey. Today, it has grown into a two-story building stocked with a wide variety of grains, nuts, dried and fresh fruits, produce, spices, and dairy products. It has more business than it can handle.
>
> There are three reasons why this Co-op is successful:
>
> 1 Its prices are low.
> 2 It serves a unique function: providing organic foods which are hard to find elsewhere.
> 3 It is deeply involved with the community it serves.

This last category still represents some problems. The storefront with its crudely painted sign, front window crammed with notes, posters, and with an endless trail of long-haired young people, is a little nervous-making for the poor blacks, Indians, and ordinary lower-middle-class folks in the neighborhood. Nevertheless, one 70-year-old woman who lives on a $170/month Social Security check said: "Things have been a lot easier for me since I found this store. It's close and the food is good and cheap."

The North Country Co-op has a point of view. It decided to sell simple, nutritious unprocessed foods: grains, flours, dairy products, dried fruits, nuts, honey, peanut butter, spices, herbs, fresh vegetables, and fruits. Meat is not part of their point of view and is not considered an essential part of the diet—thus, it is not sold. No canned goods are handled because of packaging waste and use of preservatives.

North Country buys grains and dried foods in bulk. Customers bring their own bags and jars, serve themselves, weigh and price their own purchases, and total their own bills. A 10% markup covers the co-op's operating expenses.

The Co-op obtains most of its raw grains—corn, millet, wheatberries, and soybeans—direct from "organic" farmers. The store saves money buying right from the source this way *and* the growers receive more for their crops than they would get on the regular market.

They have brought inexpensive food and organizational focus and other dollars-and-cents benefits to the Minneapolis-St. Paul area. Perhaps more important, though, is the feeling of a community spirit that the store is helping to build.

ECOLOGY FOOD CO-OP
Store: 201 North 36th Street
Warehouse: SW Corner 33rd & Race Street
Philadelphia, Pennsylvania 19104

One of the most successful and ambitious natural health food groups, Ecology Co-op, started in February, 1970, as a buying club in Philadelphia. They bought limited supplies, once a month, from Walnut Acres, a well-established organic grain source. They have grown rapidly under good management, rent a store, and operate a stone mill. This group also has a co-op warehouse with a walk-in refrigerator to supply other co-op stores, restaurants, and buying clubs. The former manager, Ed Place, has moved on to the warehouse operation.

With the advent of a citywide co-op federation for produce and their distribution center they are now able to envision the spreading of local co-op stores throughout the city. They have about $3000 a week worth of business in dairy products and natural foods, including canned goods. And they are now about to increase their volume with the addition of new produce and new co-ops.

Non-members pay 25% markup, noncontributing members 15%, and working members 5%. Before the expanded produce operation they employed 8 workers at a minimal wage. This co-op has a voluminous catalog listing the sources of all the items. This plus order forms are given to member stores for orders through the warehouse. They were able to meet the cost of buying their warehouse by temporarily adding a 5% surcharge onto wholesale prices, until the needed amount was raised.

Ed Place feels that buying clubs and supermarkets are not the only answers to the problem of food distribution. He advocates ''a balance by which the perishable items (produce, grains, etcetera) will be distributed by the preorder buying clubs and the nonperishables will be distributed through neighborhood stores which are owned and operated by the buying clubs.''

The federation does not believe in vertical management. They make no separation between labor and management but have a uniform pay rate for all jobs and rotate responsibilities and schedules as much as possible. The management elects representatives to the board and has veto power over new employees.

The board, in turn, hires people, usually from the ranks of volunteers, on a trial basis. (Although they have never been forced to fire anyone, people have left because of irreconcilable differences in philosophy.) The federation's policy is to hire workers from the member co-ops. Each co-op has the option of sending their own people to do their share of the work or of having the federation hire someone to do it for them.

Ed Place claims that the federation ''differs from the Rochdale principle since we charge the lowest possible price and have no patronage refund. Our philosophy is to distribute solely to co-ops and to charge only the actual cost of our operation.''

The federation has plans for a capitalization fund which allows for all the member co-ops to set aside money in a special account weekly.

This will be used for capital expenditures (fixed assets). Any co-op may withdraw at any time and will be bought out by the remaining co-ops.

A suggestion from Ed Place, as given in the *Journal of the New Harbinger*, for large buying groups: "Be sure each order is prepaid one week in advance by having each family or family unit deposit their money directly into the federation's bank account."

(In this way checks would have a chance to clear before the pickup date.) This greatly reduces problems that might arise related to cash and cash flow. With the prepaid deposit system there only remains the cash-and-carry nature of the buying to be dealt with—which in some areas can be handled by putting up a cash bond for credit with wholesalers.

"With their deposit tickets as proof of payment, have the families turn in their order to one person within their family group responsible for their workload for any given week."

AUSTIN COMMUNITY PROJECT
608 Oakland Avenue
Austin, Texas 78703

What started as a "food conspiracy" with a one-day-a-week distribution, has evolved into a store, warehouse operation with paid workers, and an extensive community commitment. Over half of the members are students at the University of Texas and many others are trying to be independent craft people.

The Project, which is a federation of community cooperatives, collectives, and producing units, started early in 1972. They are attempting to bring together the people who do not want to be caught up into a purely commercial economy, and the co-op clubs and stores. Their goal is to establish a community for mutual help.

For the first six months or so, this elusive goal was put aside until they were able to establish an effective organization. Instead of relying solely on volunteers, they elected John Dickerson as a paid co-ordinator.

Until the spring of 1973, there was a period of "consolidation and doldrums." They were serving about six hundred people through nine co-op houses, four neighborhood co-ops, and several collective restaurants. They went to the San Antonio Terminal produce market twice a week and distributed everything the next day. But they were not expanding and felt that they had lost sight of their original aims.

In January of 1973, they held the ACP Cooperative Community Fair and attracted two thousand people. The more than thirty organizational exhibitors included living co-ops, the ACP producers, the bakery co-op, the Greenbriar Free School, Communiversity, Switchboard (a free information and help center), several community media groups, Ananda Marga Yoga, United Farm Workers, Direct Action, Ecology Action, and others. The fair generated a lot of new activity.

Initially they envisioned themselves as a Federation divided into three areas:

Distributors: Groups which distributed consumable goods and services (living co-ops, food co-ops, collective restaurants, etcetera).

Workers: People who worked in a warehouse, store or trucker people. Those who did not produce goods but helped in the process of bringing the goods to distribution.

Producers: Farmers and other craft workers.

They modified their thinking on this because it did not seem to help them do the job. Their ultimate goal is still in mind: "A community should produce as much of what it consumes as possible, and should gear its consumption whenever possible to what it can produce."

This philosophy is aimed at bringing greater control to their own lives and less dependence on uncertain outside forces. They have not yet achieved a truly representative and participitory democracy, much to the disappointment of the most active members.

There has been a new structural development in the Austin Project whereby members are sent out to work on farms in an effort to keep their commitment to the community.

NORTHEAST KINGDOM CO-OP
Box 272
Barton, Vermont 05822

This co-op began in 1970 as a small order group of chiefly natural foods. It was a singular statewide co-op with a few small ordering groups. At the present time, NEK is part of the larger New England Peoples Co-op (NEPCOOP's other 4 members are the Plainfield Co-op, West Lebanon Co-op, Burlington Co-op, Franklyn Co-op). Although the 5 major co-ops within the NEPCOOP organization feel a great solidarity, they do work off the decentralized concept of small, self-run volunteer consumer-ordering groups.

They are beginning to organize farmers in the area for the marketing of locally grown produce which they hope will complete the food cycle, as well as trying to maintain an organically grown level of quality. They are also trying to organize "low-income" people on the consumer basis.

The Northeast Kingdom Co-op works out of a storefront and is open 5 days a week. Having approved the NEK program, VISTA supports 4 workers (2 workers share wages). The co-op has 350 members who are "rural Vermont farmers, mill workers, homebodies, homesteaders, and townspeople."

The NEK puts out an attractive monthly newsletter printed on recycled paper. Since they have found that the 10% surcharge used to cover co-op expenses cannot also pay for newsletter costs, NEK asks its members to pay either a yearly subscription of $1.25 or 10% per issue. The newsletter includes articles, poems, recipes, letters, and co-op news, all imaginatively handled—as well as an order sheet. The NEK co-op organizes events such as softball games, picnics, rock dances, potluck suppers, and sewing and natural foods workshops.

COMMON MARKET, LTD.
1340 Washington Avenue
Madison, Wisconsin 53715

1335 Gilson Street
Madison, Wisconsin 53715

The Common Market, with its two warehouses, is part of a large network of cooperatives throughout this university town. The co-op started in February of 1971 with 10 to 20 buying groups and now has expanded to about 2800 members in approximately 150 groups.

Groups of families or individuals buy once a week with a preorder system. On Thursdays, a committee compiles a mimeographed price list for the coming week. The individual group telephones or brings in a completed master list by the following Tuesday noon. On Wednesday the lists are collated by volunteers and the food ordered for the warehouse.

On Friday a representative of each group pays for and picks up the order from the warehouse and receives a new price list for the following week. Each group lends a hand at the warehouse once a month and seems to enjoy working together while they save between 20 and 40% on their food.

Some produce comes from Freedom Farm, a black farmers' co-op in Mississippi, but the bulk of the food comes from Chicago's Water Street Markets. The baked goods come from another co-op, Nature's Bakery, with local dairies and farmers supplying additional food. Common Market tries to stock as much local and organic food as they can get. This follows the pattern that many co-ops have established: support the local small farmers, especially those who try to grow foods by organic methods, for a more natural community. They have found the price is the same as the Chicago wholesale market.

MADISON COMMUNITY CO-OP
Madison Associations of Student Cooperatives
1001 University Avenue
Madison, Wisconsin 53715

This part of the cooperative community is essentially an information center and clearing house for all the co-ops in Madison. It maintains a current list of the 24 housing co-ops as well as the co-op services and stores in the area. One of the aims of the Madison Community Co-op is to maintain the continuity of the co-ops after the first group of enthusiastic people leave or students graduate.

Jay Jacobs, one of the workers at the co-op says, "We have a pretty good idea of why co-ops fail and what can be done about it. I think co-ops should federate, consolidate management and wherever possible streamline it, engage in real management training, so that this generation of facts, figures and techniques doesn't get lost for the next generation."

In addition to the above organizations, there is the Eagle Heights Co-op with 250 members, located in the married students' housing development; the Green Lantern Eating Co-op, founded in the 1940's; two other eating co-ops: the Mifflin Street Co-op and the Whole Earth Learning Community discussed in the chapter on co-op stores.

The cooperative movement extends to other aspects of life in Madison—there are fine art and craft co-ops, book, printing, garage, bicycle, clothing, and weaving co-ops. The cooperative services include a bookkeeping co-op, (a group of treasurers and bookkeepers from various co-ops who help each other as well as other individuals). The People's Office maintains a 24-hour-a-day switchboard information center for various activities, locations of crash pads, and drug rescue programs.

This loosely-knit group of cooperatives clearly demonstrates that the cooperative idea is more than just a saving of money on food; it is an approach to dealing with the essential problems of society.

chapter 7

Direct-charge Cooperatives

Not only do we get our cold air and snowstorms from Canada, but something new and provocative has originated in the north—the "direct-charge co-op." It may very well be the solution for many of the difficulties that have plagued co-ops in this country.

While it started in Ottawa in 1964, and has proliferated across Canada, it is still so new here that most people active in co-ops have never heard of it. The real novelty lies in the policy of weekly service charges.

This ranges in different areas from $1.75 to $2.50 weekly for fifty weeks a year. (Apparently, there is a two-week vacation allowed.) The members sign a contract to maintain this fee, even if they skip weeks of shopping. There is also a modest refundable investment which can be made gradually. And one can resign with sixty days written notice.

The food is then sold at *wholesale* price. The fixed fee allows the co-op to budget the operating costs for the year or period. It does not change if the consumer buys more or less per week, but many direct-charge co-ops have flexible fees for the elderly or single members.

HUB CO-OP (MID-ISLAND CONSUMERS SERVICE CO-OP)
250 Albert Street
Nanaimo, British Columbia

A. R. Glen, the president of the Hub Co-op describes the concept:

Essentially, we have asked the members to buy shares in the co-op—to acquire land, construct a warehouse building (prefabricated steel, cement floors), install steel shelving, coolers, checkout stands, etcetera, and put in a stock of food supplies which include dry groceries, produce, bakery goods, meat—in short, most of the items that you would find in a supermarket.

Hub buys most of their supplies from a wholesale cooperative and are not at the mercy of private wholesalers. The markup of 2% covers freight and "shrinkage," while wages, power, taxes, etcetera, are covered by membership fees.

The Hub Co-op, formed in 1962 as a source of petroleum products, heating fuel and auto accessories, added a household supplies division in early 1971. This is called the "Trumart" division, which has appliances as well as a food operation. With 1830 families in the membership, the sales of food (at wholesale prices) are about $2,700,000 a year.

With the fees that amount to about $127,000 a year, they also pay seven full-time and ten part-time employees. The investment in land, buildings, equipment, and stock is now about $140,000. Instead of making this just another big business, this nonprofit co-op has enabled their members, who are the owners, to have some control of the cost of living.

Just how much of a savings they achieve has to be compared with the community. The average markup at the local chain store is 20%. After taking into account the weekly fee and the average weekly purchase, the saving for Trumart members is roughly 17%. They also do a large volume in meat and that saving is 28%, according to their latest comparison.

It may not be as slick-looking as some supermarkets, but it is clean, bright, and comfortable, and complete with a free coffee bar. This particular co-op does not have the "country store" atmosphere that many new co-op members in the U.S. want, but there is no reason that this format could not be adapted to suit needs elsewhere.

With the addition of experienced management (there is no margin for mistakes), adequate financing, and loyalty from members, they have been able to maintain a stability not often found in the new co-ops. Their method of operation will be of interest to those who wish to establish a more secure economic base for their own co-op. It should also be of interest to established supermarket co-op members because of the greater savings.

The following information is from their brochure and will give you a clear picture of their operation.

1 There are no restrictions on membership in Hub Co-op.

2 You will be asked to pay a *$2 Membership Fee*, which is paid only once, and to subscribe for eight $10 shares—a total of $82. You do not have to pay this amount all at once; just the $2 fee and one share of $10 (total $12) and give your promise to pay for the rest of the shares over a period of time as you can afford to. In the case of Trumart purchases, the 2% surcharge can go toward your shares until they are paid up. The *only exception* to the requirement that you own $80 in shares is when you intend to purchase only *petroleum products* and not groceries or household supplies. In that case, you will be asked to buy *only $40* in shares. Trumart grocery contracts are available only to members who have purchased, or have agreed to subscribe for, the full $80 in shares.

3 As a member of Hub Co-op, you are an equal *partner and shareholder* along with all the other members. You have the same rights and privileges as any other member—no more and no less. The basic principle of Hub Co-op is *"all for one and one for all"* in the true spirit of cooperation.

4 *Trumart serves only its members*, not the general public. However, nonmembers are always *welcome* to drop in, look around and get information. If you have friends who are interested, bring them along. If they wish to shop, they may do so by obtaining a *Courtesy Shopping Card* from the Manager or from one of the cashiers. This is a *one-time privilege only*.

5 The *meat-cutting* is done by *contract*, which means that the people behind the meat counter are not Trumart employees. However, Trumart controls the *quality and*

pricing, and all meat is paid for at the regular checkouts. If you wish to buy in large quantities for deep-freeze storage at home, you may make arrangements with the butcher, with payment being made to Trumart.

6 Service Fees are collected for 50 weeks in the year. You can choose any two weeks in the year when you don't wish to pay. This is to allow for *summer vacations*, etcetera, when members are away from home and can't use the warehouse. New members are asked not to exercise this privilege during the *first three months* after joining without advising the manager. If you are going to be away from the community for a longer period of time, or for other good reasons are unable to use Trumart temporarily, you may *request excusal* from the weekly fee by *consulting the manager*.

7 Trumart also operates an *Order Desk* for the purchase of major items such as *appliances*. These items are not carried in stock and the purchase must be negotiated after reference to the *wholesale catalogs*. The Trumart Purchasing Agent will make these arrangements with you.

8 Members are encouraged to make additional investments in Hub Co-op over and above the share requirements. The investment plans available are *Co-op Loan Certificates* which may be purchased for $10 each and mature in three years with interest at 6%, and *Co-op Five-year Deposit Certificates*, which offer an interest rate of 7% per annum.

9 A *General Meeting* of the members of Hub Co-op is held in September of each year, and notice of place, date and time is sent by mail along with an audited financial statement. At this meeting, each member who attends has *one vote*, regardless of the number of shares held. The purpose of the meeting is to receive the report of the *Board of Directors*, to deal with the financial statement, to decide on the disposal of the surplus for the year, and to fill vacancies on the Board of Directors. Hub Co-op is governed by a *seven-man board*, all *elected* by the membership, and they serve without pay.

In the U.S., there are scattered reports of a direct-charge co-op being developed in the New England area. The attempt is being made by a woman who formerly belonged to a Canadian group. Another report cites that several New Haven co-op supermarkets are also interested. But very little is known about this form of co-op in the U.S., outside of an interesting Los Angeles group who has adapted the concept to their own style.

ESP CO-OP
11615 Mississippi Avenue
Los Angeles, California 90025
Phone: (214) 478-1922

The ESP Co-op (Equitable Society of Pioneers Cooperatives Association) is the formidable name. The vegetarian section is also known as ESPCA. They are located in a warehouse that is open Thursdays to serve their 35 members. (Including groups or clubs, the total is about 1000 households.)

George Tucker, of the ESP Co-op, reports, "Direct-charge . . . generates enormous efficiencies, is in fact a more equitable distribution of costs than a percentage markup, encourages loyalty to the Co-op . . . provides incentive."

Their aim is to create a stable, wholesale herb and natural food cooperative with national distribution, one that is consumer-oriented. Their feeling is that the existing, traditional cooperative suppliers are too producer-dominated.

George Tucker says, "The only way co-ops will work together effectively and develop a strong national movement is by developing a mutual trade relationship. The direct-charge method may provide the means."

Essentially, ESP has two separate operations: they supply produce, herbs, naturally grown food including meat and grains as well as other groceries for local household members, and they also ship herbs, spices, herbal products, and some natural foods to other groups.

They are particularly proud of the quality and low prices of the herb division and expect to be able to charge the lowest prices in the U.S. as they expand.

The following method of operation for the herb division is excerpted from their order form:

> ESPCA is a direct-charge cooperative association owned and controlled by its customer-members. It serves no other class of owners and is therefore completely dedicated to serving members—consumers and small businesses trying to survive a world of enormous corporations. ESPCA specializes in herbs. We handle a full grocery selection for local members, but shipping costs are generally prohibitive for small orders of other items, with the possible exception of some natural foods.
>
> We try always to be below or match the lowest known West Coast price—or within a few pennies at worst. We believe we still offer the lowest average prices for most users in North America.
>
> Prices available to members only. Nonmembers may place one trial order at these prices plus 4%, plus 75¢ handling, payment in full with order. Nonmembers may always order at twice these prices, payment in full with order.

Single Households and Groups of 2 to 4 Households or Equivalent:

> Membership fee, nonrefundable one-time-only: $2.50
> Direct charge (fee): $2.00/month
> Deposit (refundable): $5.00 initially
> Direct charge and deposit payable two months in advance of current month.
> One-month trial nonmember (nonvoting) shopping: $2.00 may be used only once during any calendar year.

Larger Groups and Stores

> Membership fee: $5.00

Direct charge: $10.00/quarter (3 months)

Deposit: $5.00/quarter if *sales* of products which could be obtained through ESP at competitive prices are less than $1000 a month. Otherwise somewhat more and negotiable after the first quarter.

Deposit and direct-charge payable one quarter in advance of current quarter (i.e., $35 due with first order).

Competitive prices f.o.b. West Los Angeles. Free local delivery.

Minimum order is fifty cents (50¢)!

Returns only for good cause (our fault) and only with prior authorization.

Unless you specify a maximum price for a given item, we request confirmation of orders if and only if the *total* cost of all items ordered and available has increased by more than ten percent (10%).

No additional service charges.

Discounts available for multiple packages of a given size. We will gladly discuss your particular packaging needs.

MARITIME COOPERATIVE SERVICES
P.O.Box 750
123 Halifax Street
Moncton, British Columbia, Canada
Att: Stefan Haley—Information Officer

The Maritime Cooperative Services, Ltd., is a federation of consumer and producer co-ops that functions as a service and wholesale organization to supply the twelve to eighteen direct-charge stores in the Atlantic Canadian area.

They offer some excellent advice to those interested. The numbers involved may seem too rich for the blood of the average co-op, but all those numbers can be graded down to suit your own needs.

One thing is certain: this is not an amateur venture and the management should be experienced in co-op operations. The direct-charge co-op form is probably more advisable for an area with a stable population (such as co-op housing units or rural areas) or when sponsored by another organization with a large membership base. The following are highlights from their manual:

Operational Costs:

A budget is prepared each year projecting all operational costs. The total is divided by the number of weeks involved and the results further divided by the number of members.

EXAMPLE:

Budget (52 weeks)	$135,200.00
Net Weekly Expense (135,000 ÷ 52)	2,600.00
Weekly Fee (2,600 ÷ 1000 members)	2.60

Quarter or monthly operational results are reviewed by the Board and interim fee change if necessary would be subject to membership approval.

Each member, by signed contract with his direct charge operation must pay the weekly fee as determined and agreed upon by the membership. We would stress this is an obligation of membership regardless of the amount of purchases made. The management objective is to operate within the agreed budget.

Capital Investment:

One of the prime factors in cooperative action is ownership and control by the people it serves. It is only natural that ownership is necessary for control and that control is essential to ensure continuous attainment of membership's objectives.

By design, a direct-charge operation produces no earnings, as savings are passed along at the time of sale. Thus, share capital investment must be made by agreed amounts in a specific manner to meet the total requirement.

EXAMPLE:

Total Capital Required	$300,000.00
Number of Members	1,000.00
Per Member Investment Required	300.00

Method—each member is required to invest $10.00 on joining and by signed contract must invest an additional $5.00 per quarter until $300.00 investment is reached (amounts may vary).

In the initial stage, borrowed monies may be used and repayment made as quarterly installments are paid.

Possible methods of obtaining initial capital:

1 Require total share investment by each member.
2 Offer short term savings certificates, interest bearing, to members.
3 Mortgage loan.
4 Combination of 2 and 3.

The Cooperative League of the U.S.A. has some other advice:

In the United States, federal income tax laws make by-law provision for patronage refunds desirable even in a "direct-charge" cooperative. Otherwise, you may not be able to deduct them from corporate income tax *if* you develop excess net earnings and want to refund. You don't have to use the patronage refund provision, but it should be there.

They also have developed a manual for direct-charge co-ops in addition to other organizational guides.

chapter 8

Low-income Cooperatives

While many chains have gradually closed their markets in ghetto areas as unprofitable, and cooperatives in black areas have failed because of poor management, bad location, or community indifference, one of the co-op supermarkets that has survived deserves special attention.

HARLEM CONSUMER'S COOPERATIVE
147th Street and Seventh Avenue
New York, New York

The Harlem Consumer's Cooperative is a totally member-financed organization that survived a rough five-year beginning. Plagued by a nineteen-month strike and harrassment finally stopped by Federal Court order. However, the unity and sheer determination of the leaders and members pulled them through. It has many solid working people and professionals as members, as well as residents just struggling to get by. The store seems to have avoided the coldness and detachment of the big city and added a feeling of community. Neighbors chat in the wide aisles and clerks greet the patrons in the spacious, pleasant supermarket.

One of the organizers and a dynamic force behind the cooperative is their lawyer, Cora Walker. Her story might be a primer for other groups determined to start a market. Here is how she remembers it:

Actually, how I got involved in it is something. I was living in Morningside Gardens Co-op when my doorbell rang and I was asked if I would work with this group. I wanted to be

involved with community work and still be in the area where
my home and youngsters were. My office has always been in
Harlem and one of the things that had been concerning me in
the sixties was the lack of involvement of the community
residents in their problems.

But there was a tremendous response from people in the
community to the concept of self-help and I was looking for
something to enable me to function in that vein. It dawned on
me that one of the things that was bad was their food. Since I
had worked with the co-op that I lived in and the co-op
supermarket that we had there, I asked that group if they
would help me get started. I found that actually, everybody
wanted to make a study, but nobody wanted to get involved.
As a result of the '64 riot I had made a commitment to the
people on the street that I would not involve myself in any
studies of the problems. I would do what I could to help them
actively start trying to resolve them.

Late in August '66, they came to me with this chap that
they were going to work with to try and get a co-op started. It
went back and forth and in December we invited the community to a meeting. We threw out to the people the concept of a
co-op supermarket in their area to find out if they liked the
idea. And they in turn overwhelmingly said yes. We told
them what a co-op was and how it functions. I suggested that
each person who was interested be given ten or twelve 3 by 5
cards where they could put their name, address, and phone
number and the fact that they were interested. Then they were
to get twelve of their friends or neighbors who were interested. Then I wanted the finished list to see if we had a
substantial group—say 500—who wanted to do something.
When he came back to me and said that we were ready to go, I
drew the incorporation papers. I think that was my doom . . .
because when you file a certificate of incorporation you have
to put your name on it. And I just didn't like the idea that my
name was on it and that it would not be a success!

After we incorporated, there was a meeting in June '67 and
this chap reported that he had $1700 and 41 members. Well,
everyone began to wonder, obviously, whether or not it was

viable. Rather than abandon the project, I tried to—maybe in the language of the people on the street—explain to them what it involved and what it meant. And Claude Brown and I got on a sound truck on street corners, and we had 17 teen-agers ringing doorbells, leaving the literature and card and explaining what it was about. If anyone was interested, they could mail or bring a check or money order for $5 here. And lo and behold, I had $10,000. We had planned on eight weeks but we did it in six.

Before I knew it, the money was coming in and I didn't know the first thing about setting up a supermarket. Then I had to try to find someone who did, and who would contract with the group to provide consultant services. Finally, the operators of the Pathmark chain agreed to be consultants and advise at the level that the people would understand.

You know, getting the money for it was the least of the problems. The thing that kept me up nights was worrying whether or not it was going to be successful. It opened June 4, 1968, with projected gross weekly sales of $32,500. In the first five days it did $48,000, and averaged $38,000 for the first nine months. So now, whether or not it was going to be a success was not a problem. We now had a commitment to provide job opportunities for people in the community. We had Robert Higgins, who was an excellent trainer, to set up an on-the-job training program. Almost from the first day of hire, the trainees were functional and could render a service. I was told that by using novices the store could go bankrupt, but instead they made three times the profit of a chain. We encourage our people after they have experience to get a job elsewhere, to make room for someone new. It would be impossible to count the people who have found a new way of life. There is no doubt that the lower pilferage rate is because of people's involvement. Every customer is a set of eyes. It's their money that they are watching.

I've been in Harlem for twenty-six years, working as a professional, and I have never seen anything that has brought the people together like this. It has become the hub of 4500 families for a positive, constructive group. We have even branched out to co-op housing, with our own construction company.

Our stockholders' meetings are held twice a year. We discuss everything—how the business functions, what are the business problems, and what to do about them. We discuss how the prices are arrived at, what makes a balance sheet, and what is an asset and what is a liability. I use that time to explain the various phases of the legal actions and what they encompass.

What kind of people are on the board of directors? *Plain—ordinary—good* people. We have had doctors and other professional people who just did not have the time. It is not because we have anything against them, but in the by-laws if you miss three meetings, you are off the board. It is not just a question of coming and sticking your head in the door and then leaving. They had a meeting Tuesday that started at seven and ended at half past eleven. In many instances its a question of my begging them to go.

Does it take a lot of my time? It's my life.

Among the poor in the cities, cooperative development has taken the form of loan associations and food co-ops while in the rural areas, produce groups such as farming and small craft co-ops become an outlet for the producer co-ops, following the same form the more established cooperatives have used for many years.

An example of this is New Communities, Inc., a land trust project of 5,743 acres in Lee County, Georgia. The land is cooperatively owned by about 20 poor black and poor white families and has been harvesting mostly organically-grown crops since 1969. The Poor People's Development Foundation, a small marketing organization buys directly from New Communities and other co-op farms to supply buying clubs and other co-ops from Washington to Boston.

Another group is the National Organic Farmers Association, a group of about 35 small farmers who would not be able to survive without a direct outlet for their harvests. Distribution is arranged for them by the New York Switchboard.

The low-income or hard-core poverty sector is not limited to the black population. The 13-state Appalachian region, a racially mixed area, has a per capita personal income 25 to 50% lower than the average for the rest of the nation.

But in the inner city, the low-income groups are generally the black, the aged, and those with language difficulties—mostly Latin Americans. Many of the people living in the ghetto areas are dependent on the small neighborhood store.

Because of their small sales, independent operators are not able to compete with chain stores in prices. The result is that those who are most in need are limited to over-priced, poor quality food. The rent in slum area private housing is frequently higher per square foot than elsewhere in the same city or some suburbs.

To counteract this situation, many buying clubs and small co-ops have developed. One of these is a club of 300 members set up as part of the Community Action Program in Long Beach, New York.

This particular group is of mixed income, since the middle-class people who stayed behind in the community also have difficulty finding good food at a reasonable cost. Some of them have joined the co-op. With a three-dollar-a-year membership fee, they are able to finance a preorder club and would like to grow into a full-fledged cooperative store.

Meanwhile, with a part-time VISTA worker to help, they are able to obtain produce and eggs. Judicious joint buying with another group in the Port Washington, Long Island, area enables them to purchase some canned goods as well.

Other small groups have formed in Harlem around the Union Settlement House with teams mostly from the area, trained and funded through the Human Resources Commission. They are set up in the basements of housing projects and, on occasion, churches.

Hopefully, these various efforts will result in educated and organized consumers willing to participate in changing the structure of the community and their own lives, even to a modest degree. Many of the people served by these small clubs are dependent on welfare checks on a bi-monthly basis and have difficulty in prepaying for their food on alternate weeks.

If the buying organization functions solely as an emergency method of obtaining cheaper food, it obviously fits an important immediate need. There may always be a core of people who need help at some time in their lives. But mixed into these communities there are also capable people with abilities that can be sharpened and utilized for their own and the general welfare. The goal is to help people help themselves through a genuine grass-roots movement. They must invest something of themselves for the project to succeed.

A cautionary note: Jack McLanahan reported in the *Journal of the New Harbinger* that the O.E.O. withdrew support from New Communities, Inc. after local business groups put pressure on county and state politicians. Unless politics and power plays are kept out, aid from government agencies or private foundations is worthless.

That is why many economic aid projects frequently do not enable low-income citizens to acquire the skills necessary for coping with their own lives; the human potential among this group is underestimated. Worst of all, when the much-needed government funds and grants are arbitrarily removed, it leaves the people no better off, and often embittered.

There are a few newly-formed food co-ops in the cities: three limited stock stores in the Washington, D.C., area (Martin Luther King Food Co-ops), another co-op in the Watts section of Los Angeles, and a few others scattered across the country. It is still too soon to tell whether or not they will succeed. One of the most comprehensive guides to establishing low-income cooperatives is presented by:

THE COUNCIL FOR SELF-HELP DEVELOPMENT, INC.
John B. Gauci, Executive Director
265 Grand Street
New York, New York 10002

The Council is essentially, "an experiment by the established cooperative movement in the greater New York area to help low and moderate income groups organize cooperatives."*

*From an address by John B. Gauci to the Consumer's Cooperative Managers Association, July 9, 1973, Biltmore Hotel, New York.

In recent years, Mid-Eastern Cooperatives (a warehouse operation) and the Federation of Cooperatives of New York have received
more than 200 requests for help in starting co-ops. A fresh approach
was needed that would enable local leaders to adapt established
market techniques to the specific needs of the community. Methods
that serve a middle-class group are not necessarily the best course of
action for low-income areas.

The new organization hopes to share the extensive experience of
the New York cooperatives in the educational and operational fields
with community groups that request help. They seek a partnership
with viable self-help programs and the established cooperative
movement.

Because they have seen so many cooperatives fail throughout the
country, the Council will become involved only if certain criteria are
met:

1 A real commitment by the members and a need felt by the
   community.
2 Competent leadership through training of some of the participants for membership on the Board of Directors and
   other committees.
3 Policy decisions made by the community or their elected
   representatives after expert advice and information is presented.
4 Council follow-up after the project is in operation.
5 Adequate capitalization, supplied in part by the community
   members, with the remainder in low-interest loans from
   outside sources.

The last requirement has been evolved from the experience of both
black and white groups, either privately or government-organized.
Whenever the necessary capital to start a self-help project has been
exclusively donated, the project fails because of lack of community
involvement.

Mr. Gauci goes on to say, ''When a community requests our help
we explain to them that our help will be of no use unless the group
takes its responsibilities seriously. We try to impress upon them that

the project is a difficult one and that they are fully responsible for it."

If the community group expresses real interest the Council will help them to organize their cooperative by offering the following services:

1 Provide a ten session training program on cooperative principles and practices and a general idea of the business aspects of operating a supermarket.
2 Prepare the required legal documents.
3 Work with the group on techniques to organize promotional campaigns in the community, to describe both the cooperative idea in general and the cooperative supermarket project in particular.
4 Prepare a budget, a sales projection, and a projected income and expense statement.
5 Prepare proposals to funding agencies and banks for the loans for the necessary capital.
6 Make recommendations for location, size of store, layout of store, building or renovating, equipment, furnishing, merchandising, inventory, and other matters related to the food supermarket business.
7 Provide training to the members of the Board of Directors, The Education Committee, The Store Committee, and other committees that may be appointed by the Board.
8 Provide the necessary training for all personnel, including managerial staff, to work in the supermarket.
9 Continue to give its assistance and advice to the Board of Directors of the Cooperative Society for *one year after the Supermarket is open for business or as long as necessary*.

At the present time, the Council is advising a few groups in Brooklyn: the Fort Greene section, the Boerum Place area, and Brownsville. It is hoped that the Brownsville Co-op, which is the one furthest along in development, will be a model for co-ops in other low-income areas.

John Gauci reports, "Brownsville represents one of the worst slums in New York City. Vacant, burned out buildings are all over. It has a population of 114,000. Sixty percent are on welfare; 14,000 are unemployed and 45,000 live in substandard houses. It is a high crime area with heavy traffic in drugs."

A successful food cooperative will be an important "boot-strap" effort in a thoroughly demoralized area. The Council was first contacted by The Brownsville Community Council, an anti-poverty group, in 1971. The Brownsville group had been trying to develop a market in the area for years.

They were under the impression that all the capital that they needed was $2,500.00, to be raised by selling 500 shares at $5.00 each. The original idea was to staff the supermarket with inexperienced people on welfare and pay them $5,000 to $7,000 annually.

The Brownsville Community Corporation called a meeting to correct the information that they had given the residents and to attempt a more realistic picture of the ramifications involved in opening a supermarket. "It became apparent that they did not enjoy the trust and confidence of the people of the community," according to Mr. Gauci.

A nucleus of about ten people persisted after that angry meeting broke up and subsequently pursued training sessions with the Council for Self-Help Development.

There are meetings once a week of the Steering Committee and any of the general public interested in attending. At these meetings methods of adapting to the needs of a low-income community are worked out.

There are other factors involved in this community: the general sense of hopelessness and apathy. John Gauci says, "For centuries poor people have been called upon to attack others, but hardly ever to join forces to build something for themselves . . . No other sector has been given less."

Unlike many other black communities, such as Harlem, Brownsville does not have a segment of middle-class people with basic organizational and office skills. Despite the tremendous effort which has gone into this project the Brownsville experiment has not yet been able to get broad financial support from the community. The Ft. Greene co-op, on the other hand, looks promising. If it succeeds, then many people ground down by poverty and hopeless despair will have gained some control of one aspect of their lives.

The following is a short survey of some low-income cooperative efforts:

ADELANTE COMMUNITY SUPERMARKET
727 Santa Fe Drive
Denver, Colorado 80204

This co-op is sponsored by the West Side Action Center, a Chicano group which runs the market on a low-profit basis and distributes the profit to the community.

CUYLER-WARREN CO-OP
460 Warren Street
Brooklyn, New York 11217

The co-op was organized as a produce-buying club in 1969 by five housewives in Gowanus, a hard-core poverty section of Brooklyn. Originally operating out of a church basement, they now have a board of directors (the five organizers), six paid workers, and a remodeled commercial garage.

With funding from the Consumers Education Action, an antipoverty program, they are able to serve this racially mixed community, including nursery schools and churches as well as individual families. The co-op has shelf stock to suit the neighborhood's daily needs and a pre-order system for meat which is distributed on Fridays and Saturdays. What started as a small buying club has become a source of high-quality food for a community, with savings up to 30%.

The ultimate aim is to develop a cooperative supermarket that will be self-supporting. At this point there is a membership drive in the community with cooperative supper parties to raise funds and acquaint the area with the operations of the store.

Many of the workers in the store have been trained by the Human Resources Administration.

ECCO FOOD COOPERATIVES, INC.
855 Genesee Street
Buffalo, New York
(Mailing address: P.O. Box 822, Buffalo, New York 14240)

The ECCO Co-op was formed in 1968 by a small group of black people interested in raising their standard of living. They started with a small storefront, a $15,000 bank loan, $5 membership fees, some financing from the Model Cities Program, and a great deal of enthusiasm.

With some of the profit of the original storefront, they were able to move into a medium-sized supermarket in March of 1973 and invest about $40,000 in the new store. At this time their volume is $18,000 a week. They trained and now employ 26 people from the community.

ECCO is able to meet competitive prices by purchasing stock from a supermarket chain operating in Buffalo. The new operation still has some difficulties involved with the first year of a larger operation. The Model Cities program offered to provide equipment. In order to take advantage of the offer ECCO moved quickly to larger quarters, without the expanded membership base needed to support such a move. As soon as they are running smoothly, the ECCO Co-op hopes to expand its membership (1000) in the community and continue the consumer education program that was formerly in operaticn.

Before they organized the store, ECCO consulted with the Ithaca Co-op (a Twin Pine supermarket) and the Harlem Co-op.

COMMUNITY BUYING CLUB/PROJECT ABLE
15 St. James Place
New York, New York 10038

This group is one of the low-income buying clubs funded by the Office of Economic Opportunity. Located in the basement area of the Alfred E. Smith housing project in the Lower East Side of New York, it is open to the community.

Vi Hinten, the director, coordinates the distribution of food and conducts the consumer education program. How to stretch food stamps and relief checks to feed large families is the greatest concern of many of the 248 members. This is not a true co-op in the way it would be if organized and run by the community, but is an excellent source of good, inexpensive food (20% cheaper than can be obtained locally). Many of the members are people with language barriers or dependent children, elderly people and those who have difficulties, in general, coping with New York.

The People's Warehouse has taken over the distribution of produce to the Community Buying Club. Dairy products are distributed twice a week. There is a 1% rebate on any purchases over $100 a year.

NEW YORK CITY TRAINING INSTITUTE
225 Lafayette Street
New York, New York 10012

An attempt to form low-income buying clubs and also educate genuine grass-roots organizers in the community started in 1971 in New York City. The Parents Advisory Council of City-Wide Head Start decided that a food co-op would be the best focus for a program to improve the inner-city environment.

It took almost a year to develop the parent organization, City-Wide Food Co-op, Inc., which serves as a central purchasing agency for small buying clubs and co-ops.

To create an effective organization with coordinated buying power in the 26 Head Start areas, consumer education and training is viewed as essential. Under the same grant that established City-Wide, the New York City Training Institute trains "Consumer Education Training Specialists."

The community specialists are local people trained in community organization, interviewing and surveying techniques, cooperative philosophy and structure, bookkeeping, and consumer education. An additional program is aimed at community residents and co-op participants.

THE PEOPLE'S WAREHOUSE
307 Bowery
New York, New York 10003

This is a new federation, still working out operational details. At the present time they have relieved Switchboard of the distribution of food from Natural Organic Farmers Association to about ten local food co-ops, forty day care centers, and low-income buying clubs.

Various members of the co-ops help staff the organization which is open about two or three days a week.

Some envision the Warehouse as just a large co-op while others see it as an organization that deals with other co-ops on a business-like level. These members would like to see it become reliable and self-supporting without going through the incredible ups and downs that many co-ops have.

Sooner or later they will find a means of working out the long-term policies, but meanwhile, the report is that prices are good. The People's Warehouse gets much needed food directly to poverty programs that have no means of transportation.

The emphasis is on dealing with the 35 nearby New England and Pennsylvania farmers who are sensitive to the ecology of the area. They are pleased to be able to distribute mostly freshly harvested produce to day care centers and co-ops, instead of fruits and vegetables that have been in refrigerated freight cars for weeks.

Many volunteer workers load the trucks up at 7 A.M. before they leave for work on Monday mornings. Others deliver the food directly to the day care centers at various places that are distribution points for the area. (The Broadway Local serves as a depot on Monday evenings for these groups.)

Although the warehouse works in the community, it mostly functions as a distribution center.

WHERE TO GET HELP

The following is a list of people, places, and publications to contact for help in setting up a low-income co-op:

CONSUMER ACTION AND COOPERATIVE PROGRAM
OFFICE OF ECONOMIC OPPORTUNITY
1200 19th Street N.W.
Washington, D.C. 20506
Publications; many programs but limited or no funds available.

CONSUMER SPECIALIST TRAINING PROGRAM
NEW YORK COMMUNITY TRAINING INSTITUTE
225 Lafayette Street
New York, New York 10022

THE COOPERATIVE LEAGUE OF THE U.S.A.
1828 L Street N.W. Suite 1100
Washington, D.C. 20036
Publications and list of co-op consultants available.

THE CORNUCOPIA, INC.
2808 West Lake Street
Chicago, Illinois 60612
Phone: (312) 722-5550
A warehouse serving low- and middle-income groups in Chicago;
   consultation.

COUNCIL FOR SELF-HELP DEVELOPMENT, INC.
John B. Gauci
465 Grand Street
New York, New York 10002
Phone: (212) 533-0710

JOURNAL OF THE NEW HARBINGER - *issue numbers 9 and 10*
Co-op Publication, Box 1301
Ann Arbor, Michigan 48104
Excellent survey of low-income/limited-resource co-ops.

FATHER ALBERT J. McKNIGHT
Southern Consumers Cooperative
P.O. Box 3005
Lafayette, Louisiana 70501

CORA WALKER
270 Lenox Avenue
New York, New York
Phone: (212) 534-6300
Available for consultation by any serious group.

chapter 9

How to Make Your Co-op Work

There are as many theories and methods of operations as there are co-ops. Your group can choose whatever elements seem the most helpful from the experience of other cooperatives. You should not have to go out and invent the wheel for yourself.

Certain procedures that work have been pioneered for you. Many nearby co-ops will welcome your helping out to get the experience directly. (You may even learn what *not* to do.)

Matthew Reich, who has worked extensively in the cooperative movement advises in *Journal of the New Harbinger*:

> To build a successful co-op requires energy for a struggle that most people are not willing to accept. It requires sustaining the enthusiasm of early organizing effort, and maintaining attitudes that are both self-critical and democratic (two concepts that go side by side).

HOW TO BUILD COOPERATION INTO YOUR CO-OP

The original founders of a co-op generally start with high hopes and spirit. Sometimes as the co-op grows, they find that they are the only members "cooperating."

Some individuals do not seem to mind, and feel that "effort given voluntarily can't be ripped off." For others, the initial hard work ends in disappointment and too frequently, the decline of the co-op. A participatory democracy is not easy, but it is still one of the best aspects and rewards of a good co-op.

The following suggestions have been compiled from the experiences of various small co-op stores, food conspiracies, and even co-op schools. They may work for you.

1 If you do not have a paid staff, you should grow slowly. Each member must understand the concept of coop-eration—how it works—before joining.

2 Jobs should be clearly defined to the new member: how long they should take, how they are done, etcetera.

3 An efficient, clearly structured mimeographed folder can be given to new members by many groups. (See the Free Venice Co-op's Orientation at the end of Chapter 3.)

Unfortunately, not all members bother to read the instructions. Also, not all the members that you may want to reach are literate. The addition of teamwork can help motivate the haphazard worker. For special groups, a volunteer guide (who speaks the same language) can keep the group effort from deteriorating and catch mistakes.

4 Limit the days open, if necessary. If you do not have a large enough, responsible volunteer staff, a storefront should not be kept open six days a week. You will be courting disaster.

5 Meetings should be held at regular intervals for problems to be worked out. If possible, prospective members should be required to attend before joining. In this way, they can judge if they want to get involved. At this time a member can learn the workings of the group and your goals.

6 Attempts should be made to use the skills and abilities of the members and community for their benefit as well as the co-op's.

Use the "heavies." This term grew because in all the co-ops there are a few hard workers who are willing to take the burden of decision and work hard. They, as well as the co-op, can flourish if they have any tact and leadership ability, by organizing teams for each chore.

Don't depend too heavily on a volunteer student staff. On or off the campus, the co-ops find their involvement is sporadic and they do move on.

Use retired people and others from the Community. They

frequently have skills and experience that are valuable. One Mill City Food Co-op member met a retired plumber on the bus who volunteered to supervise the building of their refrigerator system. Others have extended membership discounts to lawyers, nutritionists, carpenters, and accountants in exchange for professional advice.

7 You may need a paid staff, temporarily or permanently. Some dedicated workers, preferably with experience from a previous co-op, can maintain the organization until enough volunteer experience and enthusiasm is built up.

   If you have a program that VISTA approves of, they may pay for workers (See the O.E.O. office listing at the end of Chapter 8.)

   Even a paid staff should not work beyond an allotted time each week. Enthusiasm can dwindle quickly.

   As soon as possible, workers should be paid at prevailing wages. Otherwise, a destructive exploitation of a few members may build up in the co-op. It has been known to cause rancor. And that's not what a co-op is about!

8 Join forces with nearby co-ops. Your co-op can benefit from their experience.

   You can make better wholesale deals in large quantities. You can also share trucking needs.

9 Newsletters with an exchange of recipes, services, and consumer education information have been valuable tools in bringing the community together and raising the level of cooperation.

10 Your co-op should be a source of more than cheap food if it is to generate a commitment from the members. This may be one of the crucial factors in motivating cooperation.

It does not matter if you are long-haired, square, old, or young: shopping and working in a co-op should be a warmer, more human experience than at an ordinary supermarket.

It can lead to the fulfillment of ideals that have motivated participation around the world for over one hundred years: a hope for a better and more democratic social form without a profit motive.

In Harlem, the food co-op led to the rehabilitation of slum buildings, the formation of cooperative housing, and a cooperative construction company.

In the Minneapolis-St. Paul area, in addition to the ten food co-ops, a "People's Community" has developed with free clinics, counseling services, a cafe, garage, dry goods store, a food warehouse, flour and nut butter mills, a soap conspiracy, and a carpentry collective.

This vigorous young people's movement has tried to include the elderly, the large Indian population, blue-collar workers, and civil servants as well.

Throughout the country, the most cohesive groups have also had fun together. Block parties, picnics, dances, workshops and just getting to know each other—all create an atmosphere where people work better together. A co-op can be a chance to build a larger community with goodwill and mutual concern.

HOW TO DEAL WITH SUPPLIERS

Unless you are operating on a large scale *at the local produce market*, you have to pay cash. The new federations are excellent sources for many.

Check out the local distributors and wholesalers of *groceries and dry goods*. Some are listed (at the end of the book, under "Wholesale Food Suppliers."). Find out their reputation with other stores and co-ops.

Many do not like to deal with co-ops because of bad experiences with late payments or the co-ops' high rate of failure. You may have to establish your credit by prompt payments and endurance.

Speak to a few wholesalers. Sometimes they can be of great help with advice as to layout and where to find used equipment. Some have been known to loan equipment as well. You will need their services if you intend to carry any items only available from wholesalers unless you are affiliated with a high-volume warehouse operation.

You cannot deal directly with many manufacturers until you or your combined affiliates have a certain volume of business and warehouse space.

To get the best prices, you may have to pay cash and only have deliveries of a certain minimum quantity. To keep the prices low, pay promptly.

There are some questions that you should ask of a supplier. Take notes, listen to his story, read and take back a copy of his price list.

1 What are the terms—credit, C.O.D., or prepayment?
2 How is the price calculated—cost plus a standard price? Are delivery charges included?
3 Is there a minimum order for delivery?
4 Do they sell a private label brand? Is it graded?
5 What is the policy on damaged supplies, returns, and credits?
6 Do they accept food stamps or manufacturer's coupons?

Some wholesalers require a membership investment or a deposit before they do business with you. Some of these are cooperative wholesalers and your co-op will be required to send representatives to their board for management and other policy decisions. The investment might be worthwhile when your volume is sufficient.

If you are interested in a full-service store with excellent quality house brands and are near some of the regional warehouse cooperative operations that are members of the Cooperative League of the U.S.A. (CLUSA), you may be able to make some excellent arrangements. (The Family Buying Club of Flushing, Inc., is a moderate-size operation that has found this arrangement satisfactory.)

Associated Grocers (AG) is another form of cooperative supply source for many of the local profit-making supermarkets in the country. They require a deposit or fee.

These market sources are listed at the end of the book.

For those that are interested in other types of supplies such as grains, honey, and cheeses, see Chapter 6 on the New Federations.

HOW TO CUT COSTS

1 Use free publicity to establish a growing membership. Interesting releases or telephone calls to establishment newspapers, local radio stations, underground and local papers, schools and churches help build a solid base and cut financing costs.

    Use new members to spread the good news by word of mouth. Give them application forms to pass around. Keep a waiting list of applications if you are expanding too rapidly. You can then maintain your base if students graduate or if there is a sudden change.

2 Don't give credit or cash checks. (This is often difficult to maintain among friends, but necessary for the co-op.)

    Don't waste the co-op's money on spoiled food. Buy carefully. Learn how to buy. (See chapters on buying hints.) Shop around for good sources and compare prices and values.

3 Buy your equipment at auctions and when small grocers go out of business. (The Broadway Local Co-op bought a used postal truck.)

4 Some nonprofit organizations are entitled to free garbage pickups from the municipality. Find the best method to incorporate for your needs in your state.

5 Keep your fixed expenses low. Become knowledgeable about running costs, records, taxes, margins *before* trouble arises. Use volunteers for bookkeeping, legal work, carpentry, painting, mimeographing, etcetera, whenever available, but make sure that they are doing a good job for the co-op.

    Investigate the use of free facilities until you are established.

6 Many suppliers will take necessary long distance calls at their expense, so call collect. Keep the use of the telephone to absolutely necessary calls.

7 Join others in trucking, accounting, and bulk buying.

8 Try a local baker's day-old bread. (Russian peasants have lived to one hundred on it.)

9 Refrigerate perishables. Don't overbuy. Keep records of what sells and how fast. (Inventory control prevents capital from being tied up too long and minimizes spoilage.)
10 Charge a few cents when a member does not supply his own premeasured jars or egg cartons. Encourage return of paper bags.
11 Customers should do their own weighing and packaging. If there is too much "slippage" of stock (in some areas the customers have been giving themselves the benefit of a little extra on the scale) you may have to package the loose items, markup for the loss, or give some assistance in weighing.
12 Deposit receipts promptly for safety. There have been enough seriously damaging robberies of co-ops to make this an important consideration. Set up an account with a local bank and ask for advice on direct deposits by blocs or locals, if you have them, or night deposits. Keep the cashbox locked, with a responsible person in charge.

In general, it is necessary to be a little "buttoned up," especially in financial matters, if your co-op is to survive. If it fails, it ceases to be the alternative possibility that has involved so many of your members. Matthew Reich reports in *Journal of the New Harbinger*:

Tragically, over 95% of the co-ops organized in this country since the first in 1845, failed within a few years. The reasons for failure are not hard to explain in general terms: poor management, lack of capital, political polarization, and personality conflicts.

Few co-ops find the line between too loose an operation, and too tight an operation—and consequently fail as institutions. Capitalism has just been doing a "better job." Failure of the new cooperative movement in this country to study and learn from the past condemns it to repeat it.

The new movement in co-ops is slowly reaching for a better way to operate and the vigor of many co-ops indicates that it can be done. Self-indulgence is being replaced by a new determination.

HOW TO HANDLE LEGAL PROBLEMS

The following suggestions, are excerpted from an article in *Lifestyle!*, by Charlie Patterson. They are suitable for a *small* co-op store.

Before your co-op becomes very large or publicizes its existence, you should check out the legality of your operations, so that you won't be shut down or fined by the health department.

1 Sales Tax. Somewhere between the farm and your table, tax must be paid on food. In some states, this tax is usually paid by the retailer. This means that when the co-op buys from wholesalers, it is legally responsible for collecting and paying the food sales tax. For this reason, most co-ops need to become "official" somewhere along the line. If you're small you don't need to worry, but if you're any sort of a public organization, beware of the law!

2 Incorporation. A food co-op can file as a nonprofit corporation. Check with your lawyer. This is provided for under the law as the incorporation of Food Clubs. Filing for corporation papers costs $5. You will need a lawyer's assistance. The legal fee for incorporation may be as much as $50 (which IS a lot).

3 Retail License. If you're going to have a co-op store or building, you will probably want a retail license. This is issued by the county health department. It's a good idea to check with them before you make any big investments, because they can shut you down faster than anyone else in town. To obtain a retail license, your building will have to have fire insurance and a health inspection. Basically, you must have adequate refrigeration, a bathroom and off-the-floor storage space . . . and no flies (a self-closing screen door should take care of this). Strictness varies with the individual inspector. Some are friendly and helpful, others act as though it's their duty to make your existence absolutely impossible. The inspection is free. Once you pass,

you must check the zoning of your building. If that's all right, you pay the city clerk $5 or $10 and get your license. If the zoning is bad (residential), you may still be able to work around it if you're a small, quiet co-op. Here, a lawyer is helpful.

4 Food Handler's Permit. If the health department wants to be particularly nasty, it can require all your "employees," which may mean all your members, to have a food handler's permit. There is a special form for this, which most doctors have. It consists of a minor physical. Some county health departments provide this free; most don't.

5 Food Stamps. Once you have your corporation papers or your retail license (or both), you can apply to the U.S. Department of Agriculture for permission to accept food stamps. Call your local branch of the U.S.D.A. for specific filing information. When you apply, *don't* take NO for an answer.

6 Legal Matters In General. Because food co-ops are generally small and informal organizations, you will find that you often receive little respect from officials. This means (1) you can get away with a lot of questionable activities without being arrested or fined (just like the big corporations!) and (2) you may be denied official sanctions that are rightfully yours. Things will go much easier if you have a lawyer on your side. (Offer one a free membership!) Lawyers have had a lot of practice dealing with the regulations you'll run into and officials have infinitely greater respect for lawyers than they do for ordinary co-op members.

7 Officers. When you incorporate, you will have to have a board of directors and officers. Responsibility is a very, very important part of a co-op. But just because someone has been elected president doesn't mean he's going to act like it. Practically speaking, a responsive, benevolent dictatorship is often much nicer than a troubled democracy.

chapter **10**

How to Buy Food for Your Co-op or Yourself

HOW TO BUY THE BEST PRODUCE

Good quality produce looks fresh. Don't bother buying produce with bruises. You will not save anything after spoilage is removed. If you are interested in economy, buy fruits and vegetables in season. Buying in bulk may enable many shoppers to afford strawberries in January.

The use of standardized grades of produce is not required by federal law. Only a few individual states require that produce be inspected and graded during the packaging process using either state or federal standards. The shield with U.S. Grade No. 1 or U.S. Fancy on the box indicates good quality, but even if the market or the farmer you deal with does use grade markings, the only way to assure top quality is by using your own educated judgment. Most fresh produce can be judged fairly well by its external appearance.

A little further knowledge about the various fruits and vegetables will give the inexperienced shopper more confidence to buy wisely for the co-op. Another point: packers should handle items carefully.

Most fruits can be kept refrigerated for two to five days. Grapefruits, oranges, lemons, limes, and melons—one or two weeks.

The U.S. Department of Agriculture provides excellent bulletins which describe in detail how to buy fruits and vegetables (as well as canned goods and frozen produce).

EGGS

Like canned and frozen produce, grading for eggs is voluntary for those who request it and are willing to pay the fee. Eggs are graded according to interior quality and the condition and appearance of the shell. They should be refrigerated if they are not going to be delivered to the consumer promptly. The egg white will thin with changes in temperatures. Also, another tip—shell color does not affect the quality or nutritional value of the egg.

Grade AA or Fresh Fancy: The egg yolk is small and compact. The white is thick and the yolk is firm; both should stand high.

Grade A: The egg covers a slightly larger area than the Grade AA. The white is fairly thick and high, but like Grade AA the yolk is firm and high. Both Grade AA and Grade A are good for all purposes especially frying and poaching where appearance is important.

Grade B: These eggs are good for general purposes—cooking and baking where appearance is not so important.

Sizing: Egg prices vary according to size within each grade category. Generally, if the price difference between consecutive sizes is less than 7 cents, the better value is the larger-size eggs, providing they are in the same grade.

Jumbo	Minimum weight per Dozen 30 oz.
Extra Large	Minimum weight per Dozen 27 oz.
Large	Minimum weight per Dozen 24 oz.
Medium	Minimum weight per Dozen 21 oz.
Small	Minimum weight per Dozen 18 oz.
Pewee	Minimum weight per Dozen 15 oz.

DRY PEAS, BEANS, AND LENTILS

Dry peas, beans, and lentils are an excellent source of protein, and therefore a food bargain. They provide more protein than most other foods when combined with the protein from foods of animal origin.

Almost all peas and lentils and about one third of all beans are inspected and federally graded. Grade is usually determined by: shape, size, color, damage, and amount of foreign material. If you think that you will be saving money by buying lower grades of peas, beans, and lentils, just remember that the lower grades contain more foreign material.

When buying these dry products, look for the following federal grades which will assure you that you are getting the finest quality for your money:

U.S. No. 1: for dry whole or split peas, lentils, and black-eyed peas (beans).

U.S. No. 1 Choice Handpicked: (or Handpicked) for Great Northern, pinto, and pea beans.

U.S. Extra No. 1: for lima beans, large and small.

Instead of a federal grade you may find a state grade on the product. State grades are comparable to federal grades, and also assure the buyer of good quality. In case your source does not have dry beans, etcetera, that carry a grade, here are some helpful tips when making a purchase:

1 Look for a bright uniform color. Lack of color usually indicates loss of freshness.
2 Look for uniformity of size. Peas, beans, and lentils that vary in size will cook unevenly since small beans cook faster than large.
3 Avoid beans with cracked seed coats, insect damage, or a seemingly large quantity of foreign matter. They indicate poor-quality.

DAIRY PRODUCTS

Many dairies offer ''dock pick-up.'' You may be able to save 20% to 25% if you can go to the dairy yourself.

Cheese can be obtained in 10-pound quantities from food wholesalers or some large cheese stores will sell bulk quantities at a discount.

An article in *Lifestyle!* advises:

> Before carrying milk or eggs that are not from an au-
> thorized, licensed dealer, talk to the health department about
> laws regarding their sale. Remember that once you are offi-
> cial you can be sued—and that is no joke!

NATURAL FOODS BUYING HINTS

Brown Rice: (unpolished rice with outer shell removed) The inner
shell contains some fat and can become rancid. Brown rice retains
more vitamins and minerals than white rice. Use within 3 to 4 weeks
or refrigerate in a closed container. Should have even kernels without
cracks.

Whole Wheat Grains and Flour: Also have whole kernel which can
become rancid. Whole wheat has more vitamins and minerals than
white processed flour. Use same storage process as brown rice. Keep
covered to keep out insects.

Buckwheat Grains: They are disease-resistant and seldom sprayed.
They can be bought or ground to various coarseness to suit use. Best
in hearty winter dishes. Same storage process as brown rice.

Breads: (without preservatives): Sell and use within two days,
otherwise freeze or refrigerate to prevent molds.

Brown Sugars: Either crystallized from raw sugar or made from white
sugar with added molasses or other chemicals.

Molasses: It is a by-product of sugar cane treated with chemicals.
Raw sugar, brown sugar, honey, refined cane sugar, and turbinado
have almost no nutritional value and are high in calories.

Jams and Preserves: All contain sugar unless the absence is specifically stated on the label. Some list honey as a sweetener but unless the
label states that it has no sugar—it has sugar as well.

Vitamins: Many co-ops no longer stock vitamins for various reasons: it is the most expensive way to get the nutrients you can get from good, unprocessed food; vitamin pills are drugs; A and D vitamins are fat-soluble and excess is stored in body and can cause serious toxic reactions; the others are water-soluble and are out of the body in about two hours.

Mineral pills: Many co-ops no longer stock them: they can throw the mineral balance of the body off; some can cause dangerous side effects. Best natural sources are: good whole grains, fruits, vegetables, and meat.

Iodized Salt: If you live in an area with no seafood or a low iodine content in the water, it is advisable to use iodized salt to reduce the chance of thyroid disease. Otherwise, you do not need more additives in your food.

DNA, Yeast, RNA: Many health food suppliers list these items for sale, but *they can be dangerous*. They increase the uric acid content of the blood and can cause kidney stones or gout in some individuals. Yeasts properly belongs to the making of breads and beer.

The following is good advice from *Lifestyle!* on buying organic food:

Non-Perishables: Organic food need not cost any more than chemically treated food. If you're paying more for organic food wholesale than supermarket prices for regular food, then someone (other than you) is doing something wrong. The best way to bring prices down is by refusing to buy until you like the deal you're offered.

Produce: You should be very careful of "organic" produce at inflated prices. Ask for lab analysis by an independent laboratory. If the firm hasn't already done this, how do they know it's "organic"? Just because you don't spray for a year doesn't mean your stuff is free of chemicals which is what "organic" is supposed to mean.

chapter 11

How to Buy Meat

There are fine butcher shops (all over) that specialize in prime meat and sell between $100 and $250 worth a week, to telephone customers that they never have seen. The meat is beautifully trimmed, marbled, and, as you have guessed, costs its weight in gold.

The rest of us have to be a little more ingeneous to keep up our meat-eating habits. This requires some skill and knowledge of the wholesale cuts or bulk carcasses, what they are called, and how they should look.

This should not be too difficult for a public that has mastered highly technical comparison shopping of automobiles before making a large investment. Meat and poultry now fall into that high-cost category and should be bought with the same care.

On occasion, the local supermarket has a special on a particular cut of meat. If the cut is one that you want to use and the quality is good, it is worthwhile to stock up.

If you have room in your freezer, this can be a good buy. Supermarkets frequently sell meat as a "loss leader" in order to bring you into the store. Once you are there, they count on your buying the other items with a higher profit margin as well.

Even in the supermarket, you can get more for your money, with an understanding of what is a good cut of meat and how it should be used.

A small buying group for meat, similar to a produce-buying club, has operated with some success in an apartment building in New York City. The members, who all live in the same building, or nearby, place their order for "wholesale cuts" of meat with a butcher that specializes in orders of this sort.

The dealer is not a true wholesaler because he cuts and wraps the meat. No matter what quantities of meat they purchase, a club cannot approximate the true wholesale cost, because of the need for service. The cutting of meat into portions is a skill that must be paid for in the final cost of the purchase.

Nevertheless, by buying in large quantities, you can get better meat for less money. This club managed to get prime cuts, which are usually found only in the best restaurants and at the same price or less than the local supermarket with equivalent quality.

They order five or ten pounds of veal scallops at about two-thirds to half the price of the local butchers and supermarkets. The veal is of fine quality and they can get either shoulder or leg cuts. The latter has less gristle and is somewhat higher in price.

The scallops are sold in boxes of five pounds each and many restaurants buy their veal in this manner. At the same time, the club orders other cuts of steaks, ground steak, and lamb.

No one member of the group knew what the wholesale cuts of meat were called. It took a bit of scrambling about to find the names of their favorite cuts so that they could order properly.

Another member reported, "The dividing up is a bit messy and we needed a scale. It is much easier when someone just orders a whole cut of meat."

Another member, Margaret Turner said, "We ordered our meat by telephone every two weeks because none of us had large freezers. The price was right and the quality generally excellent."

The group had a bit of trouble until they were able to find a reliable butcher.

Until that time they had the same difficulties that the average shopper has buying meat individually. Several times the meat was not aged to the proper tenderness and once the first cut of all the rib roasts was removed.

At this point, they are all pleased with the arrangement because two of the members have become knowledgeable about judging meat. They are also satisfied with the "semi" wholesaler that they now deal with.

BUYING BULK MEAT

The American housewife today spends at least one-third of the family budget on meat, and with inflationary prices, she can soon expect to pay more. Buying in bulk cannot always be equated with saving money, and buying meat in bulk can actually be more expensive if all the factors are not taken into consideration.

Only with a careful comparison of costs among the alternatives can the question, "Is buying bulk meat economical for me?" be answered. You or your co-op, depending on whether you plan to buy individually or as a unit, must be able to judge a good buy.

Basically, the three buying alternatives are: buying a whole carcass, side or quarter; buying wholesale cuts; or buying retail cuts. Other points to consider are savings, convenience, and service for individual buyers. How much can you store in your freezer? How much can your family eat within a reasonable period of time? What cuts do they prefer? All these are important questions to answer.

First, if you are buying in large quantities, a freezer unit is a necessity. Determine whether the freezer you are buying will make bulk-buying economical in the long run. *Consumer Reports** says, ". . . the expenses of buying and running a freezer will very likely exceed any savings that the appliance could make possible by long-term storage of foods bought at bargain prices" if cost factors such as "annual depreciation, electrical consumption, repairs, packaging materials, and interest foregone on money tied up in the purchase of the appliance and its inventory of foods" are taken into consideration.

A good rule of thumb when buying foods for the freezer is: don't buy anything that is not ten cents less per pound when purchased than the price of the same food would be if purchased at the time of consumption. This price per pound should include cutting, trimming, and packaging, which most freezer provisioners include in their price. But make sure these services are included or that by doing it yourself, it will still cost ten cents per pound less than if bought in your supermarket at the time of consumption, otherwise you will be losing money.

*"Filling the Freezer," *Consumer Reports*, November 1969.

BEEF CHART

RETAIL CUTS OF BEEF — WHERE THEY COME FROM AND HOW TO COOK THEM

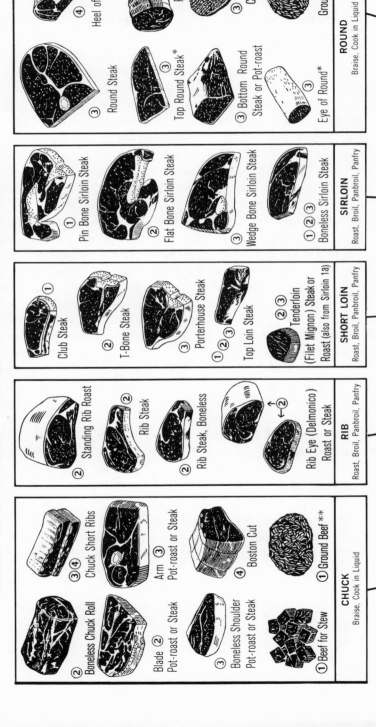

CHUCK
Braise, Cook in Liquid

- ② Boneless Chuck Roll
- ② Blade Pot-roast or Steak
- ③ Boneless Shoulder Pot-roast or Steak
- ① Beef for Stew
- ③④ Chuck Short Ribs
- ③ Arm Pot-roast or Steak
- ④ Boston Cut
- ① Ground Beef **

RIB
Roast, Broil, Panbroil, Panfry

- ② Standing Rib Roast
- ② Rib Steak
- ② Rib Steak, Boneless
- ←② Rib Eye (Delmonico) Roast or Steak →②

SHORT LOIN
Roast, Broil, Panbroil, Panfry

- ① Club Steak
- ② T-Bone Steak
- ③ Porterhouse Steak
- ①②③ Top Loin Steak
- ②③ Tenderloin (Filet Mignon) Steak or Roast (also from Sirloin 1a)

SIRLOIN
Roast, Broil, Panbroil, Panfry

- ① Pin Bone Sirloin Steak
- ② Flat Bone Sirloin Steak
- ③ Wedge Bone Sirloin Steak
- ①②③ Boneless Sirloin Steak

ROUND
Braise, Cook in Liquid

- ④ Heel of Round
- ① Rolled Rump*
- ③ Cube Steak*
- Ground Beef **
- ③ Round Steak
- ③ Top Round Steak*
- ③ Bottom Round Steak or Pot-roast
- ③ Eye of Round*

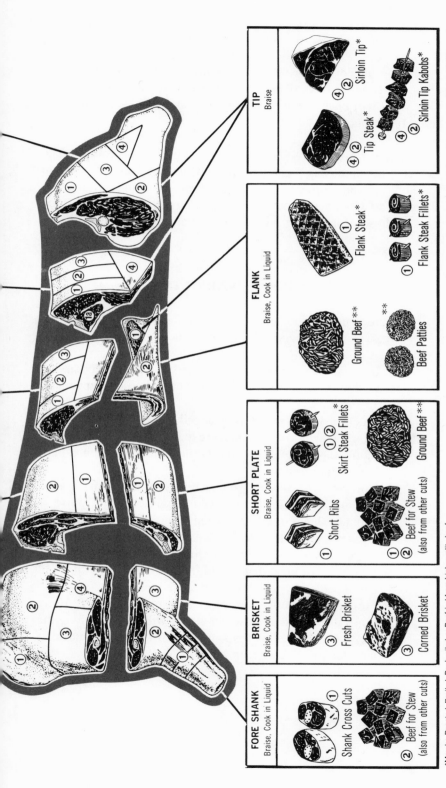

Courtesy of *National Live Stock and Meat Board*

TIP
Braise

④② Tip Steak* ④① Sirloin Tip*

④② Sirloin Tip Kabobs*

FLANK
Braise, Cook in Liquid

① Flank Steak*

① Flank Steak Fillets*

① Ground Beef** ** Beef Patties

SHORT PLATE
Braise, Cook in Liquid

①② Skirt Steak Fillets*

① Short Ribs

①② Beef for Stew
(also from other cuts)

① Ground Beef**

BRISKET
Braise, Cook in Liquid

③ Fresh Brisket

③ Corned Brisket

FORE SHANK
Braise, Cook in Liquid

① Shank Cross Cuts

② Beef for Stew
(also from other cuts)

*May be Roasted, Broiled, Panbroiled or Panfried from high quality beef.
**May be Roasted, (Baked), Broiled, Panbroiled or Panfried.

Another added tip: for the sake of food quality, rotate your purchases. Use older buys before new. Systematic labeling is a good
idea. This will enable you to save money and still eat top quality,
flavorful meats.

Saving on a product you are unfamiliar with can be a problem. The
first step in purchasing meat is to find a dealer who has a reputation
for honesty and fairness. Your local Better Business Bureau or
Chamber of Commerce may be helpful. Buyers should be warned
against those dealers who would take advantage of their inexperi-
ence.

GENERAL WARNINGS

There are many devious practices that some butchers and, sometimes, freezers provisioners employ to keep their profit margin high.

1 It is not uncommon for meat dealers to add unnecessary fat
   to chopped meat or blood to enhance its color and general
   appearance.
2 Much of what is sold as chopped meat, consists of trim-
   mings and cuts of meat that are too unsightly from deterioration to be displayed. You should watch your selection of
   meat being ground.
3 Unless you are buying from an honest man (and many are),
   you may find that the meat you bought under the guise of
   being fresh has in actuality been frozen and defrosted when
   it did not sell last week. This can be dangerous. Once meat
   is frozen and defrosted, deterioration is hastened.
4 Be careful of meat that is sold frozen. Many times it is old
   and discolored, which can affect the taste.
5 Prewrapped poultry is another item to be wary of. Many
   times if business is slow, a butcher will try to prolong the
   life of his chicken by freezing and defrosting it or masking
   its odor by soaking it in a vat of lemon juice.

BUYING WHOLE CARCASSES, SIDES, OR QUARTERS:

The USDA and FTC warn consumers to be on guard against dealers who practice the game of "bait and switch." These dealers will encourage you into the store with advertisements for U.S. Prime or Choice meat at drastically low prices.

When you get to the store and see the meat, it will be fatty and wasteful. Also rather a shock. The dealer then may say, "You don't want to give *that* to your family. Wait, let me show you something better." Of course, it is at a much higher price per pound.

Also beware of substitution. Dealers have been known to exchange cuts from the forequarter for the hindquarter cuts or to substitute lower grades of meat for higher. Employees of meat establishments boast of selling the same carcass to ten different customers—each being assured that he/she was getting that particular piece of meat.

One last tip: Buy with caution from suppliers who sell "beef bundles" or "steak packages." Inquire as to the grade and the kind and amount of various cuts.

Above all, since you cannot always stand guard over the butcher as he cuts and packages the meat, it is important that you buy from a dealer you can trust. Beware of advertisements that offer "something for nothing." No dealer can afford to give his product away, and a reputable one does not pretend to.

When you buy a whole carcass or side, it is important to remember that you will be getting a wide variety of cuts, some of which your family does not normally eat. Another important consideration is waste. Don't be taken in by advertisements which advertise superior cuts at drastically low prices because beef carcasses are sold by their gross weight.

This includes all the fat that is normally left behind on the butcher's block when you buy from a supermarket. Cutting loss can account for up to 20 to 30% of the total carcass weight. According to the USDA, generally the percentages should look like this: 25% waste, 25% ground beef or stew meat, 25% steaks, and 25% roasts.

Buying a quarter introduces another factor. The hindquarter and forequarter yield different cuts of meat. A hindquarter has more steaks and roasts, but will cost more per pound than a forequarter and yield less usable meat. A forequarter of beef has the delectable rib roast, but the other cuts are more suitable for moist cooking.

How does it all work for the individual purchaser? One example is a family of six in the Los Angeles area that have made bulk meat purchases since 1968. They have it down to an easy and pleasant routine.

Every three or four months Bill or Julie calls a semi-wholesale butcher they have dealt with for years. They place an order for a prime hind quarter of beef, a lamb and pork, loins, about three weeks before the date they intend to pick it up. Julie says, "The Los Angeles supermarkets don't carry aged meat, for some reason. We also like prime quality steaks and that is impossible to get in our area."

They watch the meat cut and wrapped to their specifications. It takes about a half hour at the butcher, about an hour of travel time and about $200 to $300. Not only do they have the quality of meat they want, but the two or three hundred pounds of meat lasts three months. The meat is immediately placed on the quick freeze shelves of their freezer, after the packages are labeled and dated.

Julie has shopped around for chickens and bought them when they have been "specials" at the local supermarket.

BUYING WHOLESALE CUTS

Wholesale cuts can be economical if you are not interested in all the cuts in a quarter. For instance, you can buy a beef short loin from which you get porterhouse, T-bone and club steaks. Consult the carcass charts to see the retail cuts that come from the wholesale cuts. Most whole cuts are bought from locker and freezer provisioners who also sell sides and quarters. Sometimes, they may even be purchased from a local butcher.

One buying club found a local butcher that gave a discount for their large order. A member said, "We felt that it was too much trouble to divide the meat ourselves. This butcher wraps each order separately."

They felt that the convenience of having a butcher close by who will also package their orders individually, worthwhile. There is still a savings because the butcher has a $500- to $700-order that he can plan on.

BUYING RETAIL CUTS

The third alternative, retail cuts, enables buyers to purchase only the particular cuts they prefer and to limit the amount of money that they spend at one time. One drawback is that you must wait for these cuts to go on "special" which may not always be convenient. Also remember that these purchases will have to be rewrapped for long term storage whereas this service is usually included in the price when buying wholesale. The price of wrapping paper or foil should be taken into account.

A good idea when considering buying meat whether it be a side, quarter or wholesale is to use a worksheet. Figure this way:

1 The total cost.
2 By pound, list the cuts of take-home meat. (What is the total weight?)
3 Figure cost per pound of the take-home meat.
4 Compare the costs of the same cuts bought other ways.

Now are you really saving money?

HINTS FOR COOPERATIVE BUYING

Buying meat cooperatively is a large task which involves a lot of time, work, and effort. Responsible and experienced members must be dispatched often to select meats, whether it be whole carcasses, sides, or wholesale cuts, if each member does not own a large freezer unit. These meats can be quick-frozen by the dealer and promptly distributed to insure wholesomeness and palatibility.

Many meat co-ops find it necessary to shop once a week. One large buying club in the Boston area, the Mission Hill Co-op, has a volunteer "meat person" who checks meat prices each week. He

USE A WORKSHEET

MEAT BOUGHT BY QUARTER, HALF, OR SIDE

How Purchased	Take Home Cuts	Pounds Take-Home Cuts
		_____ lbs.
		_____ lbs.
_____ lbs. at _____ ¢		
Total Cost $_____		Total _____ lbs.

Cost per pound, take-home meat _____ ¢

SAME CUTS BOUGHT BY WHOLESALE CUT

How Purchased	Take Home Cuts	Pounds Take-Home Cuts
_____ lbs. at _____ ¢		_____ lbs.
		_____ lbs.
Total Cost $_____		
		_____ Total lbs.

Cost per pound, take-home meat _____ ¢

SAME CUTS BOUGHT RETAIL

Cuts	Weight in Lbs.	Cost per Lb.	Total Cost
		_____ Total	_____ Total

Cost per pound, take-home meat _____ ¢

Courtesy of Extension Service,
Colorado University

then reports to the buyers where the bargains can be found.

Mission Hill has also compiled a small list of "do's and don't's" which may be helpful to co-ops starting out on the meat-buying venture.

1 When the meat is delivered, refrigerate it. Start meat breakdown after all the produce has been sorted.

2 At the time of delivery, identify, separate, and clearly label the ground chuck and the hamburger so they don't get mixed up during the breakdown.

3 Make sure the knives and your hands are clean. Use a plastic bag as your glove or mitt to breakdown meat items.

4 Pack meat orders in plastic bags. Mark the bag with the poundage and the member's number, using a permanent marker pen which will write on plastic. Label ground chuck and hamburger.

5 Put the meat orders for a member in a separate box or bag clearly labeled with the member's number. Keep this box or bag for meat only. (This makes double-checking meat much easier.)

6 On refrigerators—clearly its best if meat can be refrigerated most of the time. However, there can be foul-ups: Don't forget to pass out meat at the end of the day. Be careful not to mix up orders.

LEARN THE USDA GRADES

All meat and meat products that cross state lines are federally inspected. This assures the buyer that the meat is healthy, processed under sanitary conditions, and properly labeled. Look for a round stamp, "U.S. Inspected and Passed" to indicate that meat has passed this inspection.

Meat and meat products that are not shipped out-of-state are required by the Meat Act of 1967 to have been inspected either by State officials or locally, using standards that are comparable to those of Federal inspection.

In addition, many meat packers use the government meat grading program administered by the Department of Agriculture. This service is voluntary and the cost is borne by the meat packers. The grademark is shield. Only meat that has been inspected can be graded, so the carcass of meat you buy may only have a grade shield. But it must have one or the other—or both.

It is imperative that you as a buyer familiarize yourself with the characteristics associated with each grade of meat so that you may get the best quality (depending on each individual grade) for your money. Quality characteristics relate to the palatability of the cooked meat and to the appearance of the cuts.

USDA Prime: Ultimate in tenderness, juiciness, and flavor. It has abundant marbling. (Illustrated)

USDA Choice: Very tender, juicy, and flavorful. Less marbling than prime but still of high quality. (Illustrated)

USDA Good: Relatively more lean than higher quality, but lacks marbling which enhances flavor and juiciness.

USDA Standard: Very little fat, fairly tender. Because of its absence of marbling, it is mild in flavor and dry unless cooked with moist heat.

USDA Commercial: Produced from mature animals, it has abundant marbling, but lacks tenderness. It must be cooked slowly with moist heat to make it tender. When prepared in this manner, it can be delicious and economical.

Another important consideration when buying is the yield grade —the yield of usable meat from a carcass. This can vary greatly regardless of the quality of the meat within each quality grade category. The difference is due to the amount of outer fat on the carcass. USDA has established yield grades to measure this—Yield Grade 1 being the highest yield and Yield Grade 5 the lowest.

Learning how to select meat wisely is economically important to everyone. A thorough knowledge of the product plus hard-core buying experience are the best weapons against foolish and wasteful buying. Wise selection is the key.

Meat is judged on three main factors: conformation, quality, and cutability. Unless the supplier uses both yield and quality grades, a buyer must rely solely on his or her own judgment. If your supplier does use grades, it is still imperative to know what to look for.

Quality attributes considered to be of value include:

1 Maturity.
2 Marbling.
3 Texture of the lean.
4 Firmness of the lean and fat.
5 Color of the lean.

All of these with the exception of maturity may be appraised by

Yield of Retail Cuts as Percent of Carcass Weight for Choice Beef by Yield Grades

Retail Cut	Yield Grade 1	Yield Grade 2	Yield Grade 3	Yield Grade 4	Yield Grade 5
Rump, Boneless	3.7	3.5	3.3	3.1	2.9
Inside Round	4.9	4.5	4.1	3.7	3.3
Outside Round	4.8	4.6	4.4	4.2	4.0
Round Tip	2.7	2.6	2.5	2.4	2.3
Sirloin	9.1	8.7	8.3	7.9	7.5
Short Loin	5.3	5.2	5.1	5.0	4.9
Blade Chuck	9.9	9.4	8.9	8.4	7.9
Rib, Short Cut (7″)	6.3	6.2	6.1	6.0	5.9
Chuck, Arm Boneless	6.4	6.1	5.8	5.5	5.2
Brisket, Boneless	2.5	2.3	2.1	1.9	1.7
Flank, Steak	.5	.5	.5	.5	.5
Lean Trim	12.3	11.3	10.3	9.3	8.3
Ground Beef	13.3	12.2	11.1	10.0	8.9
Kidney	.3	.3	.3	.3	.3
Total Percent Salable					
Retail Cuts	82.0	77.4	72.8	68.2	63.6
Fat	7.6	12.7	17.8	22.9	28.0
Bone	10.4	9.9	9.4	8.9	8.4
Total	100%	100%	100%	100%	100%

viewing the rib eye. This particular portion of the carcass is quite useful since it will indicate the quality of the entire animal. A high quality rib eye will lack large amounts of muscle bundles and their connective tissues (gristle). It will be firm, fine-textured, and have a bright cherry-red color. Marbling should be visibly abundant, but at the same time fine-textured and uniform.

It is also important to judge the maturity of the carcass. Youthful beef will naturally be more tender and juicy than beef that is older. To estimate maturity, look at the split dorsal processes of the vertebrae.

Ossification, in this case, the change of the vertebrae into bone will first appear in the sacral region at the base of the vertebrae. In a young carcass, the sacral vertebrae (lower back) will show distinct separation while in an older animal it will fuse into a single bone.

Also the cartilages on the end of the thoracic vertebrae (the area between the neck and the abdomen) will be completely cartilagenous if the carcass is young. If the carcass is old, they will be in the process of ossification or ossified. One other method of appraising the age of the meat is to look closely at the lean. If it is dark and coarse, the animal is likely to be older.

ADDITIONAL HINTS FOR BUYING A CARCASS

The next factor, *conformation*, refers to the general form or outline of the carcass, its muscular and skeletal systems. Superior conformation results in thick backs with full loins and ribs, deep, plump rounds, thick shoulders, and short necks and shanks. Variations are related to the ratio of the bone to the lean.

Also important is the *"finish"* of the carcass. Fats should be firm and brittle rather soft and oily. The color of the fat is generally not considered. Yellowed fat does not have any effect on the grade.

Cutability is the amount of usable meat on the carcass. This factor is normally covered if a yield grade stamp appears on the carcass. Otherwise, you are left to your own judgment.

Look for an animal with a minimum of fat covering and kidney, pelvic, and heart fat. The muscling should be thick which is usually indicated by the rib eye. The following step will help you roughly

LAMB CHART

RETAIL CUTS OF LAMB — WHERE THEY COME FROM AND HOW TO COOK THEM

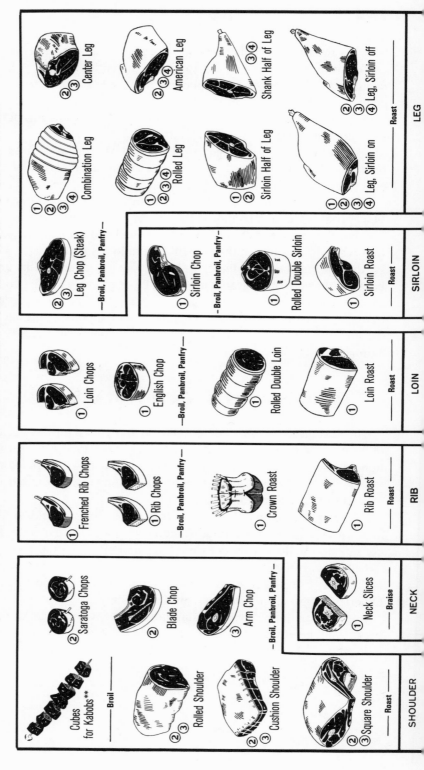

LEG

- ②③ Center Leg
- ②③④ American Leg
- ③④ Shank Half of Leg
- ②③④ Leg, Sirloin off
- ①②③④ Combination Leg
- ②③④ Rolled Leg
- ①② Sirloin Half of Leg
- ①②③④ Leg, Sirloin on
- ②③ Leg Chop (Steak) —Broil, Panbroil, Panfry—
- —— Roast ——

SIRLOIN

- ① Sirloin Chop — Broil, Panbroil, Panfry —
- ① Rolled Double Sirloin
- ① Sirloin Roast
- —— Roast ——

LOIN

- ① Loin Chops
- ① English Chop —Broil, Panbroil, Panfry—
- ① Rolled Double Loin
- ① Loin Roast
- —— Roast ——

RIB

- ① Frenched Rib Chops
- ① Rib Chops —Broil, Panbroil, Panfry—
- ① Crown Roast
- ① Rib Roast
- —— Roast ——

SHOULDER

- ② Saratoga Chops
- ② Blade Chop
- ③ Arm Chop — Broil, Panbroil, Panfry —
- Cubes for Kabobs** —— Broil ——
- ②③ Rolled Shoulder
- ②③ Cushion Shoulder
- ②③ Square Shoulder —— Roast ——

NECK

- ① Neck Slices —— Braise ——

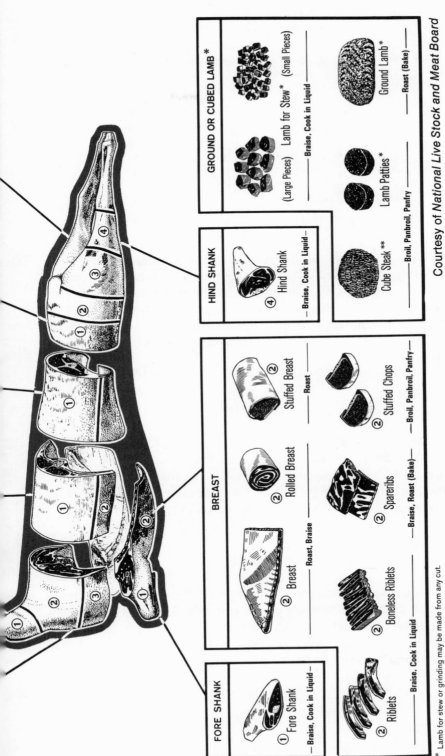

FORE SHANK

① Fore Shank
— Braise, Cook in Liquid —

BREAST

② Breast
— Roast, Braise —

② Rolled Breast

② Stuffed Breast
— Roast —

② Riblets
— Braise, Cook in Liquid —

② Boneless Riblets
— Braise, Cook in Liquid —

② Spareribs
— Braise, Roast (Bake) —

② Stuffed Chops
— Broil, Panbroil, Panfry —

HIND SHANK

④ Hind Shank
— Braise, Cook in Liquid —

GROUND OR CUBED LAMB *

(Large Pieces) Lamb for Stew* (Small Pieces)
— Braise, Cook in Liquid —

Ground Lamb*
— Roast (Bake) —

Lamb Patties*
— Broil, Panbroil, Panfry —

Cube Steak **
— Broil, Panbroil, Panfry —

Courtesy of National Live Stock and Meat Board

* Lamb for stew or grinding may be made from any cut.
** Kabobs or cube steaks may be made from any thick solid piece of boneless Lamb.

determine the yield grade until you are experienced enough to judge by sight:

Thickness of fat over rib eye	Preliminary Yield Grade
.2''	2.5
.4''	3.0
.6''	3.5
.8''	4.0
1.0''	4.5

While all these attributes—quality, conformation, and cutability—may be used in assessing beef, pork, veal and lamb carcasses, the emphasis of each varies with the type of meat. Veal, for instance, lacks marbling within the lean and is therefore less firm than beef. It also has less fat than comparable grades of beef. Consequently, the texture of the fat and the distribution differ with each meat variety.

LAMB

Lamb can be judged exactly like beef, right down to the quality check of the rib eye. In young lamb, the lean is generally a light color and gives the impression of being moist and fine-textured, whereas the lean of older lamb (yearling mutton and mutton) is darker. Young carcasses have a milder flavor and are more tender.

PORK

Pork is usually sold in wholesale or retail cuts, but if you find a supplier who deals in whole carcasses or sides look for a modicum of fat. (Approximately one inch of uniformly thick backfat for a 140-pound carcass.) The fat should be firm, not oily. High quality ham has a firm, fine textured surface and a bright greyish-pink color.

The lean should be marbled. Do not buy hams whose lean meat looks coarse and stringy.

POULTRY

Poultry, like meat must be inspected if it is to cross state lines. It may also bear a grade shield, either A or B. The U.S. grades apply to five kinds of poultry—chicken, turkey, duck, goose, and guinea hen. Poultry must be federally inspected for wholesomeness before it can be graded for quality. U.S. Grade A poultry is full fleshed and meaty. It is well finished and attractive in appearance. Grade B poultry is still of excellent quality but, it lacks meatiness and is less attractive.

The tenderness of poultry depends on the age (class) of the bird. Younger birds are more tender than older ones. If the poultry is not young, the label will carry the words, "mature" or "old." Also the skin of the bird will be whitish-yellow rather than a true bright yellow. The younger birds are best for frying, boiling, and roasting, while older poultry is well suited and economical for stews, soups, and salads.

Young Chickens: Rock Cornish game hen, broiler, fryer, roaster, or capon.

Young Turkeys: Fryer-roaster, young hen, or young tom.

Young Ducks: Duckling, broiler duckling, fryer duckling, or roaster duckling.

PORK CHART

RETAIL CUTS OF PORK—WHERE THEY COME FROM AND HOW TO COOK THEM

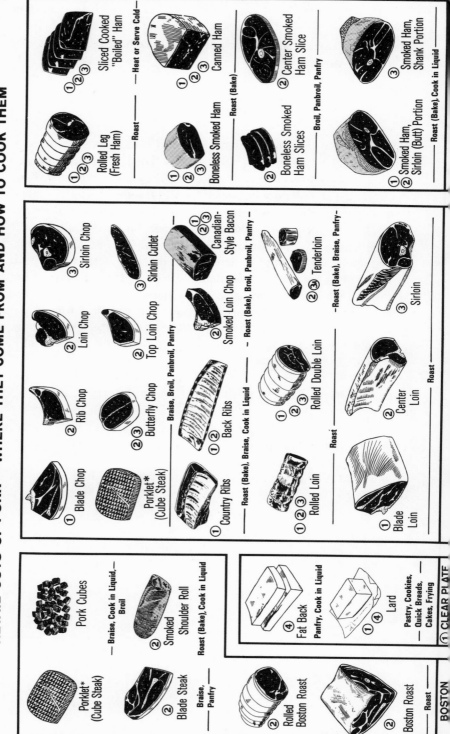

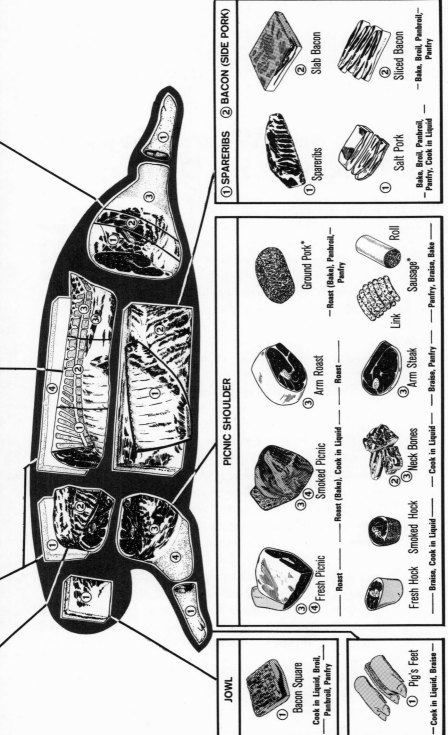

① SPARERIBS ② BACON (SIDE PORK)

② Slab Bacon

② Sliced Bacon

— Bake, Broil, Panbroil,—
Panfry

① Spareribs

① Salt Pork

Bake, Broil, Panbroil,
— Panfry, Cook in Liquid —

Courtesy of *National Live Stock and Meat Board*

PICNIC SHOULDER

Ground Pork*

— Roast (Bake), Panbroil,—
Panfry

Roll

③ Arm Roast

———————— Roast ————————

Link   Sausage*

③ Arm Steak

———— Braise, Panfry ———— Panfry, Braise, Bake

③ ④ Smoked Picnic

——— Roast (Bake), Cook in Liquid ———

② ③ Neck Bones

———————— Cook in Liquid ————————

③ ④ Fresh Picnic

Smoked Hock

Fresh Hock

Roast ——— Braise, Cook in Liquid ——— Braise, Panfry ——— Cook in Liquid

JOWL

Bacon Square

Cook in Liquid, Broil,
— Panbroil, Panfry —

① Pig's Feet

— Cook in Liquid, Braise —

*May be made from Boston Shoulder, Picnic Shoulder, Loin or Leg.

chapter 12

How to Buy Wine or Supplies for Making Your Own

With the recent upsurge in popularity of wine, many people are looking for new sources of inexpensive wines. Unfortunately, with the new import taxes and the decreased value of the dollar, most acceptable imported wines are too expensive for daily use. There are some modestly priced wines grown in the United States, but it will be about two years before there are enough high quality grapes harvested in California to approximate some of the wine from French vineyards and still sell for a moderate price.

Meanwhile, for those who have developed a taste for wine without the pocketbook to go with it, here are a few suggestions:

1 Try California wines in gallon or half-gallon sizes. After you have opened the bottle you pour the remainder into clean, smaller bottles or soda bottles with tight screw tops.

2 For those who like a semi-sweet wine with a more pronounced taste, New York State wines may be agreeable. They are not suited to everyone's palate, but many prefer the distinctive taste. The vineyards that grow grapes similar to European varieties will not be in large scale production for a number of years. At this time the wine from these special vineyards are still relatively expensive, though less costly than imports.

3 Buy directly from a small vineyard that does not distribute its stock through retail outlets. There are a few of these vineyards in the Sonoma County section, north of San Francisco. The prices are going up because of the increased demands and the newly expanded vineyards will not be in

full production for two to three years. Since September of 1973, the following vineyard has been able to ship some mail orders. Their stock is limited but good:

TIBURON VINTNERS `ᵌ
Windsor Vineyards
Sonoma County, California 95492

4 Learn how to buy inexpensive imported wines. Since this requires a book in itself, I would like to recommend *Alexis Bespaloff's Guide to Inexpensive Wines*.* This book will also enable the average purchasers to thread their way through the incomprehensible forest of wine labels. There is also a chapter on the proper storage and the serving of wine.
5 Buy wine by the case. This generally will result in a 10% savings. You must have storage space with an even temperature unless you expect to use the case within a few months.
6 Make your own wine. Unless you have high standards, this is the cheapest method of all. Many people have been making their own wine for years. The United States government allows you to make 200 gallons a year, but do not try to sell any. Note: For some reason there is still a 1916 law on the books, that states it is illegal to make wine at home if you are single. In addition, one must be the head of the family, in residence with people related by blood or marriage. Free permits can be obtained from any district office of the Bureau of Alcohol, Tobacco, and Fire Arms, of the United States Treasury Department.

Access to the California grapes will give a better quality and cheaper wine, although some people use dried elderberry or other fruit.

Alexis Bespaloff's Guide to Inexpensive Wines, by Alexis Bespaloff, New York: Simon and Schuster, 1973.

There is good information on how to make your own wine—as well as tasting sessions for those who make their own wine—at Home Winemaking and Brewing (address below).

Many co-ops have stocked these materials and directions, but for those interested (individuals or co-ops) write to:

HOME WINEMAKING AND BREWING
1140 University Avenue   2030 North Main Street
Berkeley, California 94702   Walnut Creek, California 94596

FERRATA WINERY
1120 West 15th Street
Escondido, California 92025
Not organically oriented but old-time producers of their own wine, vinegar, and all juice.

NICHOLS HERBS AND RARE SEED CATALOG
NICHOLS GARDEN NURSERY
1190 North Pacific Highway
Albany, Oregon 97321

WINE TABLE
1214 South Park
Madison, Wisconsin 53715

Bibliography

A Brief Guide to Natural Food Co-ops. Washington, D.C.: The Cooperative League of the U.S.A.

Board and Committee Manual. Washington, D.C.: The Cooperative League of the U.S.A.

Co-op Stores and Buying Clubs. Washington, D.C.: U.S. Government Printing Office, 1972.

Cooperatives, U.S.A.—Facts and Figures. Washington, D.C.: Cooperative League of the U.S.A., 1972.

Cosline, Hugh. *An Adventure in Cooperation*. Ithaca, N.Y.: Cooperative Consumer Society, Inc.

Danforth, Art. *Co-op Depot Manual*. Washington, D.C.: The Cooperative League of the U.S.A., 1970.

————.Ours! *How to Organize a Consumer Cooperative*. Washington, D.C.: The Cooperative League of the U.S.A., . 1971.

Dodge, Philip J. *A New Look at Cooperatives*. New York: Public Affairs Committee, Inc., 1972.

Filling the Freezer. Mt. Vernon, N.Y.: *Consumer Reports*, November, 1969.

Food Cooperatives, 2nd. ed. Philadelphia: Food Conspiracies, 1972.

Freezer Meat Bargain, Consumer Bulletin #5, Washington, D.C.: Federal Trade Commission.

*Goohane, Frank, Jr. *Since Silent Spring*. Washington, D.C.: Consumers Union special publication, 1970.

Journal of the New Harbinger, Volume II, #s1, 4 & 9. A Journal of the Cooperative Movement. Ann Arbor: North American Student Cooperative Organization.

Lambert, Paul. *Studies in the Social Philosophy of*

Cooperation. Washington, D.C.: The Cooperative League of the U.S.A., (out of print).

Lifestyle #1, October, 1972. Unionville, Ohio: The Mother Earth News, Inc.

*Magnuson, Warren, and Carpenter, Jean. *Dark Side of the Marketplace*. Washington, D.C.: Consumers Union special publication, 1968.

Margolis, Richard J. *The New Leader*. Special Issue, April 17, 1972. New York: American Labor Conference on International Affairs, Inc.

Margolius, Sidney. *Health Foods—Facts and Fakes*. New York: Walker and Company, 1973.

Meat Buys For Your Freezer. Extension Service Pamphlet #48. Fort Collins, Colorado: Colorado State University.

Meat Evaluation Handbook. Chicago: National Livestock and Meat Board. 1969.

Neptune, Robert. *California's Uncommon Markets*. Richmond, CA.: Associated Cooperatives, Inc., 1971.

Primer of Bookkeeping.

The Mother Earth News #4. Unionville, Ohio: The Mother Earth News, Inc.

Time to Organize?

WIN Volume VIII, #12. Rifton, New York: WIN Publishing Empire, July, 1972.

You Asked About Co-ops. Washington, D.C.: The Cooperative League of the U.S.A.

USEFUL REFERENCES FOR TECHNICAL AID, BOOKS AND PAMPHLETS

CONSUMER REPORTS, also ANNUAL BUYING GUIDE
256 Washington Street
Mt. Vernon, New York 10550

*With the exception of listings with asterisks, all publications are available at The Cooperative League of the U.S.A., 1828 L Street N.W., Washington, D.C. 20036

THE COOPERATIVE LEAGUE OF THE U.S.A.
1828 L Street N.W. Suite 1100
Washington, D.C. 20036 (202) 872-0550
Provides list of pamphlets, manuals, and books. They are varied
    and interesting. They also have a list of 200 to 300 co-op consul-
    tants.

FEDERAL EXTENSION SERVICE
U.S. Department of Agriculture
Washington, D.C. 20250
Many local offices

FEDERATION OF SOUTHERN COOPERATIVES
40 Marietta Street Northwest
Atlanta, Georgia 30303

GOVERNMENT PRINTING OFFICE
Washington, D.C. 20420
Provides list of technical aids for small business

JOURNAL OF THE NEW HARBINGER
P.O. Co-op Publications
Box 301
Ann Arbor, Michigan 48106
A journal of the cooperative movement—a bi-monthly publication of
    North American Students Cooperative Organization. The associa-
    tion also has an excellent list of publications.

MINNESOTA ASSOCIATION OF COOPERATIVES
55 Sherburne Avenue
St. Paul, Minnesota 55103

SMALL BUSINESS ADMINISTRATION
U.S. Department of Commerce
Washington, D.C. 20416
Field offices in major cities

SUPERMARKET INSTITUTE
200 East Ontario
. Chicago, Illinois 60611
Technical and training material

WISCONSIN FEDERATION OF COOPERATIVES
122 West Washington Avenue
Madison, Wisconsin
This is a coalition of co-ops of all kinds, throughout Wisconsin. The
    Federation does management training, fosters educational pro-
    grams, and sponsors lobbying for legislation favorable to coopera-
    tives.

Names and Locations of Cooperatives

If you cannot reach one of the co-ops listed, try to reach another large co-op or federation nearby. They can generally furnish a list of co-ops in your vicinity.

The asterisk (*) indicates that a description of the co-op appears in the appropriate chapter.

Co-op supermarkets have been omitted because they can be located in the local yellow pages.

ARIZONA

Rough Rock Black Mesa
   Enterprise
Rough Rock Demonstration
   School
Chinle, Arizona 86503

Ganado Feed and Consumer
   Co-op
P.O. Box 767
Ganado, Arizona 86505

Na-Ah-Tee Co-op Inc.
Indian Wells Rural Branch
Indian Wells, Arizona 86031

Kosmic Gardens
2234 North 24th Street
Phoenix, Arizona 85008

Blue Gap Food Cooperative
Pinon, Arizona 86515

Dineh-Bi-Naa-Yei Cooperative
P.O. Box 566
Pinon, Arizona 86510

Gentle Strength Co-op
38 East 5th Street
Tempe, Arizona 85281

The Granary
526 North 4th Street
Tucson, Arizona 85700

People's Food Co-op
612 South 4th Street
Tucson, Arizona 85700

Tood-Dine Benalyebahowan
Star Route, P.O. Box 410
Winslow, Arizona 86047

ARKANSAS

Eureka Springs Food Co-op
4 North Main Street
Eureka Springs, Arkansas 72632

Ozark Food Conspiracy
347 North West Street
Fayetteville, Arkansas 72701

CALIFORNIA

Alhambra Peoples Cornucopia
3082 West Main Street
Alhambra, California 91801

Altadena Food Co-Op
3737 Canyon Crest Road
Altadena, California 91001

Bell Gardens Buyers Club
and Community Service
P.O. Box 2160
Bell Gardens, California 90201

Head Start Food Co-op
5713 Florence Place
Bell Gardens, California 90201

Berkeley Food Conspiracy
1317 Cornell
Berkeley, California 94709

Free School Bus
2400 Ridge Road
Berkeley, California 94709

Organic Food Association
Berkeley Food Conspiracy
2326 Sacramento Avenue
Berkeley, California 90202

Carson Natural Foods Co-op
c/o The General Store
21808 Avalon Boulevard
Carson, California 90745

Pitzer Food Coop
Box 452, Pitzer
Claremont, California 91711

Orange County Food Conspiracy
1880 Whittier Street #B
Costa Mesa, California 92627

Santa Cruz Consumer's Co-op
P.O. Box 54
Davenport, California 95017

Davis People's Food Coop
TB-15, Campus
University of California
Davis, California 95616

Alternative Distributing Co.
6448 Bay Street
Emeryville, California 94608

Wholewheat Food Co-op
c/o Isla Vista Community
   Building
Isla Vista, California 93017

Divide Community Action
   Council
P.O. Box 11
Kelsey, California 95643

Laguna Beach Ecology Club
2137 Laguna Canyon Road
Laguna Beach, California 92651

Beach Organic Foods Co-op
1747 East 2nd Street
Long Beach, California 90802

Long Beach Food Conspiracy
1747 East 2nd Street
Long Beach, California 90802

Poor and Simple Food Co-op
3322 East Anaheim
Long Beach, California 90815

Sunset Beach Food Co-op
P.O. Box 4272
Long Beach, California 90804

Ecology Club of Laguna Beach
1360 Glenneyre
Los Angeles, California 92651

*ESP Co-op/The Good Herb
P.O. Box 295
Los Angeles, California 90025

The Gathering
4506 South Western Avenue
Los Angeles, California 90062

Immaculate Heart Co-op
Immaculate Heart College
2021 North Western Avenue
Los Angeles, California 90027

Los Angeles Natural Foods
   Co-op
6665 1/2 Franklin Avenue
Los Angeles, California 90068

Operation Recapture
701 West 34th Street
Los Angeles, California 90007

Oriental Food Co-op
c/o Oriental College
P.O. Box 0
Los Angeles, California 90041

*Westside Co-ops
11973 Dorothy Street
Los Angeles, California 90049

Beach Area General Store
3837 Mission Boulevard
Mission Beach, California

Monterey Co-op
616 Lighthouse
Monterey, California 93940

Palo Alto
1285 Dale Avenue
Mountain View, California
  94040

Oakland Food Co-op
c/o Peoples Food Market
5520 College Avenue
North Oakland, California
  94618

Valley State Food Co-op
19044 Parthenia Street
Northridge, California 91324

Edible Dry Goods Conspiracy
363 62nd Street
Oakland, California 94618

The Fourth Estate
P.O. Box 11176
Palo Alto, California 94306

Palo Alto Coop/Sunnyvale Food
  Conspiracy
422 Palo Alto Avenue
Palo Alto, California 94301

Pasadena Natural Foods
1625 East Walnut
Pasadena, California 91106

Shasta County Consumers
  Association
1125 Butte Street
Redding, California 96001

Redondo Beach Food Co-op
131 Paseo De La Concha
Redondo Beach, California
  90277

*Consumers Co-op of Berkeley
Main Office: Information
4805 Central Avenue
Richmond, California 94804

Golden Hills Co-op
1625 Fern Street
San Diego, California 92102

Mission Beach General Store
3837 Mission Boulevard
San Diego, California 92019

Ocean Beach Peoples Store
4859 Voltaire
San Diego, California 92107

San Diego Co-op
1649 7th Avenue
San Diego, California 92101

Bernal Heights Community
  Co-op
320 Winfield
San Francisco, California 94110

Common Good Buying Club
1259 46th Avenue
San Francisco, California 94122

Common Market Buying Club
Haight Ashbury Food
  Conspiracy
1446 Cole Street
San Francisco, California 94117

Community Food Club
2590 Sacramento Street
San Francisco, California 94115

Eat Good Buying Club
1310 Haight Street
San Francisco, California 94117

Eucalyptus Club
440 10th Avenue
San Francisco, California 94118

Eureka Valley Food Chain
4529 18th Street
San Francisco, California 94114

Free Food Co-op
41 Nevada Street
San Francisco, California 94110

Grouphead Buying Club
977 Clayton Street
San Francisco, California 94117

Haight Food Conspiracy
284 Frederick Street
San Francisco, California 94117

Healthy Hunza Buying Club
233 Brunswick Street
San Francisco, California 94112

Inner Mission Co-op
837 South Van Ness
San Francisco, California 94110

Inner Sunset Food Co-op
24 Irving Street
San Francisco, California 94122

Naturally Good Buying Club
  No. 1
200 Cherry Street
San Francisco, California 94118

Naturally Good Buying Club
  No. 2
787 22nd Avenue
San Francisco, California 94107

Ongoing Picnic Co-op
2234 20th Avenue
San Francisco, California 94116

PFP Food Co-op
417 Lawton Street
San Francisco, California 94122

Rose Hips Buying Club
107 Noe Street
San Francisco, California 94114

St. Peter's Food Buying Club
1200 Florida Street
San Francisco, California 94110

San Francisco Food Buying
  Program
239 Vienna Street
San Francisco, California 94112

Seaside One Buying Club
1370 40th Avenue
San Francisco, California 94122

Seeds of Life
3021 24th Street
San Francisco, California 94110

Western Addition Food Buying
  Club
457 Haight Street
San Francisco, California 94117

White Panthers Food Conspiracy
599 Ethel Avenue
San Francisco, California 94100

Zen Co-op
319 Page Street
San Francisco, California 94102

Dominguez Hills Food Co-op
1516 West 19 Street #C
San Pedro, California 90732

San Pedro Food Co-op
715 North Meyler
San Pedro, California 90731

Integral Yoga Institute
311 Oceanview Avenue
Santa Cruz, California 95060

Kresge Food Co-op
Kresge College University of
  California
Santa Cruz, California 95060

Santa Cruz Consumer's Co-op
527 Seabright
Santa Cruz, California 95062

Peoples Food
503 North Pacific Coast
  Highway
Solana Beach, California 92075

Volunteers in Asia, Inc.
P.O. Box 4543
Stanford, California 94305

Sylmar Buying Club
13589 Herron Street
Sylmar, California 91342

Topanga Canyon Food Co-op
19988 Observation Drive
Topanga, California 90290

Free Venice Co-op
440 Venice Way
Venice, California 90291

Organic Food Family
22 Thornton Avenue
Venice, California 90291

Van Nuys Food Co-op
5835 1/2 Woodman Avenue
Van Nuys, California 91401

Natural Foods Store Co-op
P.O. Box 371
West Pint, California 95255

COLORADO

US, Too Inc.
Colorado State University
  Extension Service
27 East Vermijo
Colorado Springs, Colorado
  80903

*Adelante Community
  Super-market
727 Santa Fe Drive
Denver, Colorado 80204

*Common Market of Colorado
1100 Champa
Denver, Colorado 80204

Divine Light Mission
1560 Race Street
Denver, Colorado 80206

Eastside Action Center Buying
  Club
2420 Welton Street
Denver, Colorado 80205

Rocinante Grocery Store
Gardner, Colorado 81040

Peoples Market
132 7th Avenue #4
Greeley, Colorado 80631

Federation of Southern
  Colorados
Peoples Enterprises
122 Spruce Street, P.O. Box 76
Lajara, Colorado 81140

Forty Thieves
96 Pike Street
North Glenn, Colorado 80233

CONNECTICUT

North End Community Action
  Consumers Co-op
183 North Main Street
Ansonia, Connecticut 06401

Charter Oak Terrace Buying
  Club
46 Sunshine Drive
Hartford, Connecticut 06106

Sheldon-Charter Oak Buying
  Club
150 Willys Street
Hartford, Connecticut 06118

Stowe Village Cooperative
66 Hampton Street
Hartford, Connecticut 06120

Food Co-op
139 Carlisle Street
New Haven, Connecticut 06519

New Haven Food Co-op
425 College Street
New Haven, Connecticut 06511

New Haven Food Co-op
490 Greenwich Avenue #1
New Haven, Connecticut 06519

Middletown Co-op
113 College Street
Middletown, Connecticut 06451

P.O. Box 555
Wesleyan Station
Middleton, Connecticut 06457

Stratford Counseling Center
2730 Main Street
Stratford, Connecticut 06497

N.O.W. Buying Club
c/o New Opportunities for
    Waterbury
769 North Main Street
Waterbury, Connecticut 06704

DELAWARE

Wilmington Cooperative Natural
    Food Club & Back to the Earth
    Natural Foods
Concord Pike
Wilmington, Delaware 19810

DISTRICT OF COLUMBIA

Stone Soup Educational Food
    Center
1801 18th Street, Northwest
Washington, District of
    Columbia 20009

FLORIDA

Alternative Vittles
1478 Gulf to Bay
Clearwater, Florida 33515

De Land Buying Club
259 West Voorhis Street
De Land, Florida 32720

Our Daily Bread
1214 Northwest 5th Avenue
Gainesville, Florida 32601

Sunshine Cooperative
    Association, Inc.
P.O. Box 115
Edison Center Station
Miami, Florida 33151

4435 Northwest Second Avenue
Miami, Florida 33151

New Smyrna Beach Buying Club
608 Washington Street
New Smyrna Beach, Florida
    32069

Sunshine People's Co-op
4811 Caesar Way South
St. Petersburg, Florida 33712

*Sunflower Natural Foods Store
1551 Main Street
Sarasota, Florida 33577

Produce Co-op
12103 North 52nd
Tampa, Florida 33617

GEORGIA

New Morning Food Co-op
862 Rosedale
Atlanta, Georgia 30306

Sun-Mec Buying Club
c/o Sun-Mec Neighborhood
    Service Center
71 Georgia Avenue Southwest
Atlanta, Georgia 30315

HAWAII

Kaiua Country Food Store
2357 South Beretaina Street
Honolulu, Hawaii 96814

People Not Profits
Nuama House
2930 Nuama Road
Honolulu, Hawaii 96819

Way Inn Co-op
P.O. Box 527
Kealakekua, Hawaii 96750

Garden of Eden
1910 Vineyard
Wailuku, Maui, Hawaii 96793

IDAHO

Co-op
c/o Good Food Store
112 East 2nd Street
Moscow, Idaho 83843

Garden Cooperative
c/o South Central Community
    Action Agency
P.O. Box 531
Twin Falls, Idaho 83301

ILLINOIS

Metro East Co-op
4 West C Street
Belleville, Illinois 62221

People's Food Co-op
1004A West Washington
Bloomington, Illinois 61701

Main Street Market
901 East Main
Champaign, Illinois 61820

*Association of Food Co-ops
4652 North Kenmore
Chicago, Illinois 60640

Community Thrift Clubs
4035 South Michigan
Chicago, Illinois 60653

*Cornucopia
2808 West Lake Street
Chicago, Illinois 60612

Divine Light Food Co-op
5026 South Greenwood
Chicago, Illinois 60615

Food Co-op
Third Unitarian Church
301 North Mayfield Avenue
Chicago, Illinois 60644

Hyde Park Distribution
5655 South University
Chicago, Illinois 60637

La Gente Food Co-op
3227 North Halstead
Chicago, Illinois 60657

Northside Co-op Ministry
2507 North Greenview
Chicago, Illinois 60614

Uptown Food Co-op
1222 West Wilson Avenue
Chicago, Illinois 60640

North End Consumers Co-op
1507 North 13th Street
East St. Louis, Illinois 62205

Peoples Cooperative Buying
   Club
1015 Liberty
East St. Louis, Illinois 62201

Edwardsville Food Co-op
South Illinois University
Edwardsville, Illinois 62025

New World Co-ops
c/o Sheil Center Chapel
Evanston, Illinois

Macomb Community Co-op
803 Bobby Avenue
Macomb, Illinois 62455

Northside Buyers Club
410 Wayne
Peoria, Illinois 61603

Laetare Partners
326 North Avon Street
Rockford, Illinois 61103

King Harvest Food Co-op
1441 North 5th Street
Springfield, Illinois 62702

Springfield and Sangamon
   County Buying Club
1310 East Adams Street
Springfield, Illinois 62703

*Earth Foods Inc. (Earthworks)
1310-1312 West Main Street
Urbana, Illinois 61801

INDIANA

Peoples Buying Club
2502 Winter Street
Fort Wayne, Indiana 46803

Peoples Pantry
104 Maple Street
North Manchester, Indiana
     46962

Earlam Eat
P.O. Box 31
Richmond, Indiana 47374

Love Story Commune
701 College Avenue
Terre Haute, Indiana 47802

IOWA

Ames Peoples Co-op
c/o Little Read Book Shop
110 South Hyland
Ames, Iowa 50010

Good News General Store
206 Fourth Street SE
Cedar Rapids, Iowa 52401

NSA Coordinator
Coe College
Cedar Rapids, Iowa 52402

Divine Light Mission
1518 Harrison Street
Davenport, Iowa 52803

Good Earth Foods
1518 Harrison Street
Davenport, Iowa 52803

Center Co-op
753 17th Street
Des Moines, Iowa 50312

Des Moines Food Co-op
1535 11th Street
Des Moines, Iowa 50314

New Pioneer Co-op Society
518 Bowery Street
Iowa City, Iowa 52240

KANSAS

Western Wyandotte Mini Market
121 Allcutt Street
Bonner Springs, Kansas 66012

Bethel-Riverview Action Group
     Buying Club
73 South 7th Street
Kansas City, Kansas 66101

Northeast Action Group Buying
    Club
950 Quindero Boulevard
Kansas City, Kansas 66101

Rainbow Foods
3950 Rainbow
Kansas City, Kansas 66103

Total Action Group Buying Club
1620 South 37th Street
Kansas City, Kansas 66101

Hill Co-op
1539 Tennessee Street
Lawrence, Kansas 66044

Lawrence Milk Run
788 Locust
Lawrence, Kansas 66044

KENTUCKY

Berea Health Foods
408 Prospect Street
Berea, Kentucky 40403

Harlan Buying Club
c/o Harlan County Community
    Action Agency
314 South Main Street
Harlan, Kentucky 40831

Manly Area Cooperative
800 West Saint Catherine Street
Louisville, Kentucky 40222

Cumberland Farm Products, Inc.
P.O. Box 296
Monticello, Kentucky 42633

LOUISIANA

The Food Conspiracy
2175 Highland Road
Baton Rouge, Louisiana 70802

Natchitoches Area Action
    Association
Farm Program-Vegetable Co-op
P.O. Box 944
Natchitoches, Louisiana 71457

Food Co-op
c/o Switchboard
1212 Royal Street
New Orleans, Louisiana 70116

MAINE

York County Community Action
Court House Annex
Alfred, Maine 04002

Mixed Nuts
Hampshire College
Amherst, Maine 01002

Bath Brunswick Consumer
    Association
P.O. Box F
Brunswick, Maine 04011

Vernon Valley Co-op
Mount Vernon, Maine 04352

Needham Food Co-op
130 Grosvenor Road
Needham, Maine 02192

Tritown Food Association
21 Washington Avenue
Old Orchard Beach, Maine
   04064

Food Buying Co-op
University & Community
   Resource Co.
100 East Annex, University of
   Maine
Orono, Maine 04473

Good Day Food Market
343 Fore Street
Portland, Maine 04111

Portland Food Co-op
c/o Good Day Market
343 Fore Street
Portland, Maine 04111

Community Food Co-op
Southwest Community Center
372 Granite Street
Quincy, Maine 02169

Sanford Food Co-op
11 State Street
Sanford, Maine 04073

Broadway Food Co-op
99 Puritan Road
Somerville, Maine 02145

Sanford-Springvale Co-op
8 Bradeen Street
Springvale, Maine 04003

Stoughton Food Co-op
11 Horan Way
Stoughton, Maine 02072

MARYLAND

Sunshine, Inc.
1714 Fe
Baltimore, Maryland 21231

Waverly Peoples Food Co-op
3019 Independence
Baltimore, Maryland 21218

Spring Bottom Natural Foods
Route 1
Belair, Maryland 21213

School of Living
Heathcote Community
Rural Route 1, P.O. Box 129
Freeland, Maryland 21053

*Glut Food Co-op
4005 34th Street
Mount Ranier, Maryland 20812

*Greenbelt Consumers Service
8547 Piney Branch Road
Silver Springs, Maryland 20901

Community Warehouse, Inc.
8215 Flower Avenue
Takoma Park, Maryland 20012

Junction, Inc.
Old County Jail
P.O. Box 206
Westminster, Maryland 21157

MASSACHUSETTS

Allston-Brighton Food Co-op
158 Harvard Street
Allston, Massachusetts 02134

Amherst Food Co-op
24 Churchill Street
Amherst, Massachusetts 01002

*Yellow Sun Nature Foods Coop
35 North Pleasant Street
Amherst, Massachusetts 01002

Andover Co-op
Main Street
Andover, Massachusetts 01810

Arlington Food Co-op
38 Bartlett Avenue
Arlington, Massachusetts 02174

Athol Peoples Food Co-op
216 Exchange Street
Athol, Massachusetts 01331

Beverly Co-op
NSCAS
356R Cabot Street
Beverly, Massachusetts 01915

Community Consumers United
88 Elliott Street
Beverly, Massachusetts 01915

*Boston Food Co-op
*NEFCO (New England Food
    Cooperating Organization)
12-14 Babbitt Street
Boston, Massachusetts 02215

Free China Town Community
c/o G.A.C.
239 Harrison Avenue
Boston, Massachusetts 02111

Interfaith Food and Grain
490 Beacon Street
Boston, Massachusetts 02115

Peace and Beans
522 Commonwealth Avenue
Boston, Massachusetts 02215

Project Place
37 Rutland Street
Boston, Massachusetts 02118

South End Food Co-op
c/o Help Program
Boston, Massachusetts 02216

Beansprout II
80 Nottonghill Road
Brighton, Massachusetts 02135

Beansprout I
12 Douglas Street
Cambridge, Massachusetts
02139

Cambridge Central Food Co-op
3 Clinton Street #4
Cambridge, Massachusetts
02139

Cambridge Food Co-op
Red Book Store
91 River Street
Cambridge, Massachusetts
02139

Cambridgeport Food Co-op
65 Pleasant Street
Cambridge, Massachusetts
02139

Franklin Street Food Co-op
438 Franklin Street
Cambridge, Massachusetts
02139

Fresh Pond Co-op
74 Reservoir Street
Cambridge, Massachusetts
02138

Organic Foods Co-op
Longbottom Leafe Ltd.
531 Cambridge Street
Cambridge, Massachusetts
02141

Pearl Street Co-op
53 Pearl Street
Cambridge, Massachusetts
02139

Prentiss Street Co-op
73 Frost Street
Cambridge, Massachusetts
02140

Rising Earth
96 River Street
Cambridge, Massachusetts
02139

Boston College Food Co-op
Boston College
Chestnut Hill, Massachusetts
02167

Concord Food Co-op
874 Barretts Mill Road
Concord, Massachusetts 01742

Good Food Union
Woolman Hill
Deerfield, Massachusetts 01342

Yarmouth Co-op
P.O. Box 379
Dennisport, Massachusetts
02639

The People First Food Co-op
238 Bowdoin Street
Dorchester, Massachusetts
    02122

Brandywine Village Co-op
42 Trustman Terrace
East Boston, Massachusetts
    02128

Bourne Food Cooperative
40 Heritage Street
Falmouth, Massachusetts 02540

United Cooperative Society of
    Fitchburg
815 Maine Street
Fitchburg, Massachusetts 01423

Another Day Co-op
42 Maple Street
Florence, Massachusetts 01060

Actions, Inc.
Elm Street
Gloucester, Massachusetts
    01930

Great Barrington Food Co-op
c/o Community Action Project
Great Barrington, Massachusetts
    01230

Haverhill Food Co-op
Able Community Action Center
5 Vine Street
Haverhill, Massachusetts 01830

Work, Inc.
652 South East
Holyoke, Massachusetts 01040

Hyannis Food Cooperative
195 Lincoln Road
Hyannis, Massachusetts 02601

Free Co-op
22 Vine Street
Lexington, Massachusetts 02173

Lexington Food Co-op
30 Woodcliff Road
Lexington, Massachusetts 02173

Lowell Food Co-op
P.O. Box 414
Lowell, Massachusetts 01853

Lowell Food Co-op
23 School Street
Lowell, Massachusetts 01854

Lynn Co-op
6 Boynton Terrace
Lynn, Massachusetts 01902

West Somerville Food Co-op
128 Professor's Row
Medford, Massachusetts 02115

Newton Center Co-op
17 Carlton Street
Newton, Massachusetts 02158

Elliot Church Food Co-op
30 Tarleton Road
Newton Center, Massachusetts
    02159

Murray Road Food Co-op
998 Beacon Street
Newton Center, Massachusetts
    02159

West Newton Food Co-op
45 Pleasant Street
Newton Centre, Massachusetts
    02159

Scituate Food Co-op
435 Tilden Road
North Scituate, Massachusetts
    02060

Our Daily Bread
26 South Main Street
Orange, Massachusetts 01364

The Mission Hill Food Co-op
18 Lawn Street
Roxbury, Massachusetts 02020
            Or
55 Beech Glen Street
Roxbury, Massachusetts 02020

The Food Co-op
Community Consumers United
    Inc.
91 Bridge Street
Salem, Massachusetts 01970

North Cambridge Food Co-op
20 Waldo Avenue
Somerville, Massachusetts
    02143

Projects Food Co-op
Somerville Housing
Mystic Avenue
Somerville, Massachusetts
    02145

Somerville Food Co-op
16 Union Square
Somerville, Massachusetts
    02143

Columbia Point Food
    Association
20 Montpelier Road
Columbia Point
South Boston, Massachusetts
    02110

Weston Organic Co-op
87 Spruce Hill Road
Weston, Massachusetts 02193

Community Stomach Natural
    Food Co-op
197 Pleasant Street
Worcester, Massachusetts 01609

Community Stomach Food
   Co-op
Produce
33 Wall Street
Worcester, Massachusetts 01604

Crisis Center Inc.
162 Chandler Street
Worcester, Massachusetts 01609

Hard Times Food Co-op
270 Pleasant Street
Worcester, Massachusetts 01609

Worcester Food Co-op
9 Larch Street
Worcester, Massachusetts 01609

Yarmouth Food Cooperative
33 Hawthorne Road
Yarmouth, Massachusetts 02675

MICHIGAN

Ann Arbor Itemized Produce
   Co-op
908 Greene
Ann Arbor, Michigan 48104

*Ann Arbor People's Food
   Co-op
722 Packard
Ann Arbor, Michigan 48104

Ann Arbor People's Produce
1520 Hill Street
Ann Arbor, Michigan 48104

Aoxomoxa
428 Hamilton Place
Ann Arbor, Michigan 48104

Applerose
404 West Liberty
Ann Arbor, Michigan 48103

*Michigan Federation of Food
   Co-ops
Peoples Wherehouse
404 West Huron
Ann Arbor, Michigan 48103

Neighborhood Action Center
   Food Club
543 North Main
Ann Arbor, Michigan 48104

*People's Food Co-op
722 Packard
Ann Arbor, Michigan 48104

Pontiac Heights Food Co-op
Arrow Wood Trail Community
   Center
2626 Arrow Wood Trail
Ann Arbor, Michigan 48105

Food Lib Front
628 Gladstone
Detroit, Michigan 48207

Franklin Dairy Co-op
3360 Charlevoix
Detroit, Michigan 48207

Masjid
8850 Grand River
Detroit, Michigan 48204

Mother Jones Food Co-op
4531 Avery
Detroit, Michigan 48912

Three For Three Food Co-op
17714 John R
Detroit, Michigan 48203

Green Earth Food Co-op
3118 Student Services Building
Michigan State University
East Lansing, Michigan 48823

Karma Co-op of Bay City
1184 West Hampton Road
Essexville, Michigan 48732

The Circle Food Co-op
1511 Detroit Street
Flint, Michigan 48503

Flint Food Co-op
416 South Avon #7
Flint, Michigan 48503

Freemont Food Co-op
Route 2
Fremont, Michigan 49412

Eastown Food Co-op
2218 Lake Drive
Grand Rapids, Michigan 49506

Grand Rapids Food Co-op
235 Charles S.E.
Grand Rapids, Michigan 49503

California Sunshine
129 California
Highland Park, Michigan 48203

People's Food Co-op of
   Kalamazoo
Wild Bill's
   Walk-On-Water-Bakery
817 West North Street
Kalamazoo, Michigan 49007

Lake Orion Food Co-op
1230 Orion Road
Lake Orion, Michigan 48035

Marquette Organic Food Co-op
230 West Ohio Street
Marquette, Michigan 49855

Mt. Pleasant Food Co-op
Route 3
Mt. Pleasant, Michigan 48858

Munising Food Co-op
717 West Superior
Munising, Michigan 49862

Grain Train Natural Foods Co-op
311 1/2 East Mitchell #8
Petoskey, Michigan 49770

Plymouth Food Co-op
c/o Center For Young People
P.O. Box 115
Plymouth, Michigan 48170

Carrot Patch Co-op
15 Clayburn
Pontiac, Michigan 48054

Hominid Services, Inc.
1114 Doris Road
Pontiac, Michigan 48057

Sylvan Lake Food Co-op
1755 Lakeland
Pontiac, Michigan 48053

Karma Co-op
708 South Jefferson
Saginaw, Michigan 48607

Saugatuck Food Co-op
Bridge Street Curio
802 Bridge Street
Saugatuck, Michigan 49453

Oryana Food Co-op
9557 West Bay Shore Drive
Traverse City, Michigan 49684

Ypsilanti Food Co-op
604 Emmett
Ypsilanti, Michigan 48197

MINNESOTA

Sustenance Shoppe
205 North Ermina Avenue
Albert Lea, Minnesota 56007

Lake Region Enterprises
Annandale, Minnesota 55302

Far Between
310 1/2 Ormsbee Street
Big Lake, Minnesota 55309

Community Buying Club
631 East 8th Street
Duluth, Minnesota 55805

Whole Foods Buying Club
631 East 8th Street
Duluth, Minnesota 55805

Glencoe Savers Buying Club
Glencoe, Minnesota 55336

Hibbing Buying Club
P.O. Box 114A
Star Route 4
Hibbing, Minnesota 55746

Our House
Highway 15
Hutchinson, Minnesota 55350

La Crescent Buying Club
Route 2, P.O. Box 152
La Crescent, Minnesota 55947

Good Foods Store
Lengby, Minnesota 56651

Twin Lakes Budget Buying Club
Litchfield, Minnesota 55355

Community Food Store
307 South Broad Street
Mankato, Minnesota 56001

Ecology Co-op
1023 Eighth Street SE
Minneapolis, Minnesota 55414

Good Grits
15th and Spruce
Minneapolis, Minnesota 55403

*Mill City Co-op
2552 Bloomington Avenue S.
Minneapolis, Minnesota 55404

*North Country Co-operative
   People's Warehouse
2129 Riverside
Minneapolis, Minnesota 55404

People's Company
1534 East Lake
Minneapolis, Minnesota 55407

*People's Warehouse
205 11th Avenue S.
Minneapolis, Minnesota 55415

Powderhorn Co-op
3440 Bloomington Avenue S.
Minneapolis, Minnesota 55404

Seward Co-op
2201 Franklin
Minneapolis, Minnesota 55404

Southeast Co-op
8th Avenue and 4th Street
Minneapolis, Minnesota

Whole Foods
2502 First Avenue
Minneapolis, Minnesota 55404

Christ's Household of Faith
Mora, Minnesota 55051

Prairie Dog Store
Morris Campus
University of Minnesota
Morris, Minnesota 56267

Northfield Buyer's Club
c/o P.O. Box 24
Northfield, Minnesota 55057

Penny Pinchers Buying Club
Olivia, Minnesota 56277

Steele County Buying Club
c/o Dodge-Steele-Waseca
   Citizens Action Council
Owatonna, Minnesota 55060

John Salmi Memorial Co-op
Lake Cabetobama
Ray, Minnesota 56669

St. Cloud Food Co-op
Neuman Center
P.O. Box 1032
St. Cloud, Minnesota 56301

Saint Anthony Park Foods
1435 North Cleveland
St. Paul, Minnesota 55108

*Selby Food Co-op
5005 Selby
St. Paul, Minnesota 55102

Sweet Earth
420 South 3rd Street
St. Peter, Minnesota 56082

Spring Valley Buying Club
Spring Valley, Minnesota 55975

Staples Peoples Pantry
Rural Route 2
Staples, Minnesota 56479

Waseca County Buying Club
Waseca Community Center
Waseca, Minnesota 56093

Clear Lake Food Buying Club
Watkins, Minnesota 55389

Ray Community Services
Waverly, Minnesota 55390

Famine Foods
120 East 2nd
Winona, Minnesota 55987

Winona Buying Club
723 East 4th Street
Winona, Minnesota 55987

MISSISSIPPI

Oxford Consumer Cooperative
512 Jackson Avenue
Oxford, Mississippi 38655

MISSOURI

Columbia Foods Co-op
915 East Broadway
Columbia, Missouri 65201

Hace Co-op Supermarket
Howardville, Missouri 63869

Community Food Conspiracy
3800 McGee Street
Kansas City, Missouri 64109

Live Center Food Co-op
Brian McInerney
915 West 17th Street
Kansas City, Missouri 64108

Redstar Food Co-op
3130 Olive
Kansas City, Missouri 64109

West Port Food Co-op
4830 Campbell
Kansas City, Missouri 64110

Westside Food Co-op
2017 West Penway
Kansas City, Missouri 64108

Compton-Grand Meat Co-op
3504 Caroline
St. Louis, Missouri 63104

Demun Community Center Food
  Co-op
700 Demun
St. Louis, Missouri 63105

Food Buyers Association
28 Benton Place
St. Louis, Missouri 63104

Laclede Co-op
Peacock Community Center
Laclede & Ewing Streets
St. Louis, Missouri 63103

Midtown Food Buying Club
4202 Folsom
St. Louis, Missouri 63110

*Midwest Cooperating
  Consumers Association
554 Limit
St. Louis, Missouri 63130

Midwest Co-op Warehouse
c/o Lea Russell
554 Limit
St. Louis, Missouri 63130

Peoples Produce
5899 Delmar
St. Louis, Missouri 63112

Water Tower Food Co-op
4522 North 9th Street
St. Louis, Missouri 63147

Westend Food Co-op
4453 Olive
St. Louis, Missouri 63108

West Pine Neighbors Food Club
3801 West Pine
St. Louis, Missouri 63108

Community Collectives
  Combine Co-op
554 Limit
University City, Missouri 63130

Community Collectives Food
  Co-op
554 Limit
University City, Missouri 63130

Older Adults Co-op Store
554 Limit
University City, Missouri 63130

Valley Park Thrifty Food Co-op
25 Vance Road
Valley Park, Missouri 63088

MONTANA

Friendship Center Meat Buying
   Club
1503 Gallatin Street
Helena, Montana 59601

The Good Food Store
642 Woody
Missoula, Montana 59801

The New Little Food Co-op
P.O. Box 854
Libby, Montana 59923

NEBRASKA

Cornhuskers Co-op
1319 R. Street
Lincoln, Nebraska 68501

Peoples Food Co-op
3513 Holdredge
Lincoln, Nebraska 68503

Prairie Sunset
5524 South 32nd Street
Omaha, Nebraska 68107

Some Folks
1461 North 91st Street
Omaha, Nebraska 68114

NEVADA

Midway Buyers Club
Old Junior High School
Lead Street
Henderson, Nevada 89015

Action Over 55 Cooperative
1632 Yale Street
Las Vegas, Nevada 89107

Community Action Self-Help
960 West Owens Street
Las Vegas, Nevada 89106

NEW HAMPSHIRE

Valley Food Co-op
Eaton Center, New Hampshire
   03832

Franconia Food Co-op
c/o Tatwamasi Natural Foods
Franconia, New Hampshire
   03580

Nashua Food Co-op
7 Gordon Street
Hudson, New Hampshire 03051

Nesenkeag Co-op Farm
RFD 1
Hudson, New Hampshire 03051

Keen Learning Co-op
69 Washington Street
Keene, New Hampshire 03431

The Store
52 West Maine Street
Lebanon, New Hampshire
03766

Manchester Food Co-op
Operation Help Office
227 South Main Street
Manchester, New Hampshire
03102

Milford Food Co-op
Operation Help Office
Putnam Street
Milford, New Hampshire 03055

Volunteers Organized in
  Community Education
2 Shattuck Street
Nashua, New Hampshire 03060

The Big Food Buying Club
New Market, New Hampshire
03857

Up Front Organic Market
50 South School Street
Portsmouth, New Hampshire
03801

Do It Store
93 Main Street
West Lebanon, New Hampshire
03784

*New England Peoples Co-op
South Co-op
52 Main Street
West Lebanon, New Hampshire
03784

NEW JERSEY

Robert Johnston
19-D Riverview Gardens
North Arlington, New Jersey
07032

Test
Engineering Management
61 Monmouth Road
Oakhurst, New Jersey 07755

New Jersey Natural Food
  & Farm Cooperative
216 Belmont Avenue
Ocean, New Jersey 07712

NEW MEXICO

*Osha Co-op
8812 4th Street NW.
Albuquerque, New Mexico
87114

Eastern Navaho Feed Store
  Co-op Association
P.O. Box 104
Crownpoint, New Mexico 87313

Torreon Food Stamp Co-op
    Association
P.O. Box 193
Cuba, New Mexico 87103

Amigos De Salud Cooperative
P.O. Box 453
El Prado, New Mexico 87529

Acoma Food Cooperative
P.O. Box 67
San Fidel, New Mexico 87038

New Life Cooperative
218 De Fouri
Santa Fe, New Mexico 87501

NEW YORK

Co-op Store
211 Dove Street
Albany, New York 12202

South End Food Cooperative
142 South Pearl Street
Albany, New York 12202

Genesee Road
Arcade, New York 14009

*Family Buying Club of
    Flushing, Inc.
202 Rocky Hill Road
Bayside, New York 11426

1AP Co-op
112 Clinton Street
Binghamton, New York 13901

Off Center Community Store
73 State Street
Binghamton, New York 13905

Brockport Food Co-op
37 Main Street S.
Brockport, New York 14420

Bronx River Soundview
    Community Corporation
1170 Boynton Avenue
Bronx, New York 10472

Brownsville Cooperative Buying
    Club
388 Rockaway Avenue
Brooklyn, New York 11212

Consumer Act Program of
    Bedford-Stuyvesant
501 Marcy Avenue
Brooklyn, New York 11206

*Cuyler-Warren Co-op
460 Warren Street
Brooklyn, New York 11217

Mongoose
782 Union Street
Brooklyn, New York 11211

Sumner Co-op
c/o Crispus Attucks
15 Sumner Avenue
Brooklyn, New York 11206

Allentown Foods Co-op
26 Maryland
Buffalo, New York 14201

East Side Community
  Cooperative
300 Williams Street
Buffalo, New York 14204

*ECCO Food Co-operatives,
  Inc.
P.O. Box 822
Buffalo, New York 14240

Help Center
Chase Hall B-7
SUCB
1300 Elmwood Avenue
Buffalo, New York 14222

Lexington Real Foods
  Community Co-op
224 Lexington Avenue
Buffalo, New York 14222

*North Buffalo Community
  Co-op
3225 Main Street
Buffalo, New York 14214

Beaver Falls Food Buying Club
Castorland, New York 13620

Cohoes Cooperative Buying
  Club
c/o Cohoes Community Action
  Program, Inc.
98 Mohawk Street
Cohoes, New York 12047

Cattaraugus Buyers
  Cooperative, Inc.
22 West Washington Street
Ellicottville, New York 14731

*Organic Energy Co-op
68-06 Fresh Meadow Lane
Flushing, New York 11365

Fredonia Co-op
SUC, Fredonia
53 West Main Street
Fredonia, New York 14063

Grocery Co-op
7 Whitaker Road
Fulton, New York 13069

Oswego County Co-op Store
Vorheas Street
Fulton, New York 13069

Geneva Food Co-op
561 South Main Street
Geneva, New York 14456

Glenfield Food Cooperative
Glenfield, New York 13343

North Family Fair
Rural Delivery 1
Gouverneur, New York 13642

Huntington Collective
P.O. Box 81
Huntington, New York 11743

People's Town Hall Food Co-op
488 New York Avenue
Huntington, New York 11743

Consumer Protection Service
   Store
140 West State Street
Ithaca, New York 14850

Guava Jelly and
   Community of Communes
   Real Food Co-op
412 Linn Street
Ithaca, New York 14850

*Ithaca Real Food Co-op
P.O. Box 871
Ithaca, New York 14850

Lowville Food Buying Club
Lowville, New York 13367

South Lyons Food Buying Club
Lyon Falls, New York 13368

Natural Foods Co-op
12 South Second Avenue
Mt. Vernon, New York 10550

Real Food Store
53 Main Street
New Paltz, New York 12561

North Valley Buyers Club
Rural Delivery 2, P.O. Box 200
Newark Valley, New York
   13811

Aquarius Co-op
405 West 148th Street
New York, New York 10031

*The Broadway Local Food
   Co-op (Conspiracy)
718 Columbus Avenue
New York, New York 10025

Chelsea Food Co-op
349 West 20th Street
New York, New York 10011

Chinatown Food Co-op
416 Henry Street
New York, New York 10002

*Community Buying
   Club/Project Able
15 St. James Place
New York, New York 10038

Cornucopia Co-op
201 East 4th Street
New York, New York 10009

*Federation of Co-ops, Inc.
Main Office
465 Grand Street
New York, New York 10002

General Theological Seminary
  Co-op
c/o Darwin Ralston
175 Ninth Avenue
New York, New York 10019

Good Food Co-op
58 East 4th Street
New York, New York 10003

*Greenhouse Association, Inc.
466 Amsterdam Avenue
New York, New York 10024

Integral Yoga Natural Foods
227 West 13th Street
New York, New York 10011

Liberation News Service
160 Claremont Avenue
New York, New York 10025

Natural Foods Center
Room 105, Earl Hall
Columbia University
New York, New York 10027

*New York Switchboard
Washington Square Methodist
  Church
133 West Fourth Street
New York, New York 10012

*Peoples Warehouse
307 Bowery
New York, New York 10003

Saffonia
For women only
243 West 20th Street
New York, New York 10011

6th Street Co-op
518 East 6th Street
New York, New York 10009

West Side Food Buying Club
1050 Amsterdam Avenue
New York, New York 10026

Westside
P.O. Box 286
Cathedral Station
New York, New York 10025

Wholesome Foods
191 East 3rd Street
New York, New York 10009

*Wild Rice
Organic Food Cop-op
325 West 16th Street (2nd Floor)
New York, New York 10011

Ossining Community
  Cooperative, Inc.
47 Spring Street
Ossining, New York 10562

Oswego Community
  Cooperative
47 East Bridge Street
Oswego, New York 13126

Richford Pennypinchers
Richford, New York 13835

*Clear Eye and Genesee Co-op
713 Monroe Avenue
Rochester, New York 14607

Free Peoples Store
713 Monroe Avenue
Rochester, New York 14607

Sound Food Co-op
541 Lake Avenue
Saint James, New York

South Ozone Park Community
  Buying Club
14205 Rockaway Boulevard
South Ozone Park, New York
  11436

Spencer Buyers Club
Rural Delivery 2
Spencer, New York 14883

Shanti Food Conspiracy of St.
  George
104 Westervelt Avenue
Staten Island, New York 10301

Stony Brook Freedom Foods
Kelly D-300B
SUNY
.Stonybrook, New York 11790

Cheap Food Ltd.
Chapel House, Office R.
711 Comstock Avenue
Syracuse, New York 13210

Syracuse Community Food
  Co-op
278 Genesee Park Drive
Syracuse, New York 13200

Troy Peoples Co-op
279 Hoosick Street
Troy, New York 12180

Trumansberf Food Co-op
46 South Street
Trumansburg, New York 14886

Food Co-op
1502 Steuben Street
Utica, New York 13501

NORTH CAROLINA

Chapel Hill Food Co-op
38 Holloway Land
Chapel Hill, North Carolina
  27514

Chapel Hill Food Co-op
501 East Rosemary Street
Chapel Hill, North Carolina
  27514

Peoples Intergalactic Food
Co-op
c/o Associated Students of Duke
University
5091 Duke Station
Durham, North Carolina 27706

Chowan Cooperative Produce
Exchange
P.O. Box 398
Edenton, North Carolina 27932

*Country Co-op
P.O. Box 111
Pittsboro, North Carolina 27312

NORTH DAKOTA

Tochi Food Store
303 Robert Street
Fargo, North Dakota 58401

Fellowship Natural Foods
221 3rd Avenue SE
Jamestown, North Dakota 58401

Something of Value
Organic Foods & General Store
618 Northeast 3rd
Minot, North Dakota 58701

OHIO

Community Action Council
Food Co-op
230 West Center Street
Akron, Ohio 44302

Direct Order Food
717 North Exchange Street
Akron, Ohio 44302

Rosy Cheeks Community Store
459 East Exchange
Akron, Ohio 44304

Whole Wheat and Honey
Community Food Co-op
125 Westmoreland
Akron, Ohio 44304

Cincinnati Food Co-op
245 West McMillan
Cincinnati, Ohio 45219

East End Food Co-op
2624 Eastern
Cincinnati, Ohio 45202

Broadway Food Co-op
4640 Broadway
Cleveland, Ohio 44127

Crises Co-ops Cleveland
1814 West 47
Cleveland, Ohio 44102

The Food C.O.O.P.
Communities Organization of
People
c/o Hillel Foundation
11291 Euclid Avenue
Cleveland, Ohio 44106

Fremont Organization Against
  Hunger
Fremont Food Co-op
802 Literary
Cleveland, Ohio 44113

Fruit and Vegetable Co-op
North Presbyterian Church
4001 Superior
Cleveland, Ohio 44103

Glenville Afro-American Co-op
Glenville Opportunity Center
1073 East 105
Cleveland, Ohio 44108

Inner City Co-op
Hough Ave. United Church of
  Christ
65 and Hough
Cleveland, Ohio 44103

Metropolitan Co-op Services,
  Inc.
Metro Meats, Inc.
2624 Detroit Avenue
Cleveland, Ohio 44113

Near West-Side Food Co-op
3004 Clinton
Cleveland, Ohio 44113

The Food Project
1807 Coventry Road
Cleveland, Ohio 44118

Columbus Community Food
  Co-op
Wesley Foundation
2635 Glenmawr Avenue
Columbus, Ohio 43202

Golden Flower Seed Co.
431 West 6th Avenue
Columbus, Ohio 43201

Osu Food Co-op
2377 North 4th Street
Columbus, Ohio 43201

Southside Food Co-op
363 Reeb Avenue
Columbus, Ohio 43207

Twin Pines Food Co-op
3494 North High Street
Columbus, Ohio 43214

Hollywood Community Center
Food Buying Club
101 Walnut Street
Franklin, Ohio 45005

United Peoples Buying Club
606 Front Street
Greenville, Ohio 45331

Kent Food Co-op
Unitarian Church
228 Gougler
Kent, Ohio 44240

Community Food Co-op Store
c/o Lima-Allen County
  Community Action Center
Memorial Hall
Elm and Elizabeth Street
Lima, Ohio 45801

Oberlin Good Food Co-op
c/o Co-op Bookstore
37 West College
Oberlin, Ohio 44074

Painesville Food Co-op
St. James Episcopal Church
Painesville, Ohio 44077

Wisconsin Food Co-op
224 South Market Street
Wooster, Ohio 44691

Greene County Buying Club
132 North Detroit Street
Xenia, Ohio 45385

OKLAHOMA

Lovelight
755 Jenkins
Norman, Oklahoma 73069

OREGON

Ashland Peoples Food Co-op
90 North Main Street
Ashland, Oregon 97520

Forest Acres Co-op
3362 Table Rock Road
Central Point, Oregon 97501

1st Alternative
1007 Southeast 3rd Avenue
Corvallis, Oregon 97330

Growers Market
301 Lincoln
Eugene, Oregon 97401

*Willamette People's
  Co-operative
1393 22nd Street E.
Eugene, Oregon 97403

The Cracker Barrel Co-op
1640 North Highway 101
Lincoln City, Oregon 97367

Food Front Co-op
1618 Northwest 23rd
Portland, Oregon 97210

Peoples Food Store
3029 Southeast 21st
Portland, Oregon 97200

Stomache
2269 West Main
Portland, Oregon 97202

Salem Community Food Store
1635 Fairgrounds Road
Salem, Oregon 97303

Sweet Home and Neighbors
  Food Co-op
1325 North 18th Street
Sweet Home, Oregon 97386

Emily Food Co-op
4930 Coyote Creek
Wolf Creek, Oregon 97497

PENNSYLVANIA

Togetherness House
32 East Armatt
East Germantown, Pennsylvania
  19144

JFK Neighborhood Action Team
  Organization
Food Cooperative
2024 Buffalo Road
Erie, Pennsylvania 16510

Adams County Buying Club
P.O. Box 205
Gettysburg, Pennsylvania 17325

Meat Buyers Club
Westmoreland County
  Conference for
  Economic Opportunity
128 East Pittsburgh Street
Greensburg, Pennsylvania
  15601

Food Co-op H
Haverford College
Haverford, Pennsylvania 19041

Solomon Homes Marketing
  Co-op
Community Building
Solomon Homes
Johnstown, Pennsylvania 15902

Weavers Way
Carpentry and Greene Street
Mt. Airy, Pennsylvania 19119

Community Food Co-op of West
  Philadelphia
3907 Spruce Street
Philadelphia, Pennsylvania
  19104

Concerned Neighborhood Co-op
St. Davids Episcopal Church
481 Flamingo Street
Philadelphia, Pennsylvania
  19128

Cross Roads Community Center
2916 North 6th Street
Philadelphia, Pennsylvania
  19133

*Ecology Food Co-op
201 North 36th Street
Philadelphia, Pennsylvania
  19104

Germantown Peoples Food
Co-op
Germantown Community
Presbyterian Church
Greene & Tulpehocken
Philadelphia, Pennsylvania
19144

Good Earth
City Line and Conshohocken
Philadelphia, Pennsylvania
19131

Greenwich Neighbors
212 South 6th
Philadelphia, Pennsylvania
19106

Greenwich Neighbors Food
Co-op
2029 South 8th Street
Philadelphia, Pennsylvania
19148

Haripasa
4726 Baltimore Avenue
Philadelphia, Pennsylvania
19143

Life Center Food Co-op
1006 South 46th Street
Philadelphia, Pennsylvania
19143

Mt. Vernon
c/o Mt. Vernon Christian Center
Umbua and Leverington Street
Philadelphia, Pennsylvania
19128

Open, Inc.
2431 North 6th Street
Philadelphia, Pennsylvania
19133

Philadelphia Citywide Co-op
Organization
5108 Newhall Street
Philadelphia, Pennsylvania
19144

Philadelphia Food Co-op
Federation
3214 Winter Street
Philadelphia, Pennsylvania
19104

Peoples Co-op of Mt. Airy
c/o Summit Presbyterian Church
Westview and Greene Street
Philadelphia, Pennsylvania
19119

South Street Co-op
624 South 4th
Philadelphia, Pennsylvania
19147

Spring Garden Community
  Center
1812 Green Street
Philadelphia, Pennsylvania
  19136

Stonehouse
1006 South 46th Street
Philadelphia, Pennsylvania
  19143

Temple Community Food Co-op
1439 Norris Street
Philadelphia, Pennsylvania
  19122

West Oak Lane Co-op
Lamont A.M.E. Church
1500 Cheltenham Avenue
Philadelphia, Pennsylvania
  19126

West Philadelphia Community
  Food Co-op
3907 Spruce Street
Philadelphia, Pennsylvania
  19104

Wharton Center
1708 North 22nd Street
Philadelphia, Pennsylvania
  19121

Revolutionary Europe
P.O. Box 4288
Pittsburgh, Pennsylvania 15203

Semple Street Food Co-op
51 Boundary Way
Pittsburgh, Pennsylvania 15217

Horn of Plenty
Denbigh Episcopal Conference
  Center
Upper Gulph Road
Radnor, Pennsylvania 19087

Princeton Food Co-op
217 Pine Tree Road
Radner, Pennsylvania 19087

RHODE ISLAND

Alternative Food Co-op
78 Biscuit City Road
Kingston, Rhode Island 02881

Food Co-op
University of Rhode Island
Student Senate Office
Kingston, Rhode Island 02881

Family Food Co-op
David Evans
16 Prospect Avenue
Narragansett, Rhode Island
  02882

SOUTH CAROLINA

Reeder Point Buying Club
Bluff Road
Columbia, South Carolina 29209

Woodland Community Progress
   Group
Route 1, P.O. Box 353
Georgetown, South Carolina
   29440

Hampton County Buying Club
P.O. Box 706
Hampton, South Carolina 29924

Peoples Community
   Cooperative
Rivers Street Extension
Walterboro, South Carolina
   29488

SOUTH DAKOTA

Cooperative Buying Club, Inc.
1024 Quincy Street
Rapid City, South Dakota 57701

Stoneground Natural Foods
517 7th Street
Rapid City, South Dakota 57701

Black Hills Resource
   Mobilization C
c/o Meade County Community
   Center
1130 Main Street
Sturgis, South Dakota 57785

Harvest Moon Foods
9 West National
Vermillion, South Dakota 57069

TENNESSEE

The Paper Bag Co-op
East Sevier Avenue
Kingsport, Tennessee 37660

Knoxville Community Whole
   Foods Co-op
1539 Laurel Avenue
Knoxville, Tennessee 37916

Neighborhood Service Center
   Buying Club
1116 8th Avenue S
Nashville, Tennessee 37203

TEXAS

*People Buying Together
222 Varsity Circle
Arlington, Texas 76010

*Austin Community Project
608 Oakland
Austin, Texas 78703

Austin Consumers Co-op
319 Texas Union
Austin, Texas 78712

Austin Food Co-op
The Ark
2000 Pearl Street
Austin, Texas 78705

Woody Hills Food Store
1200 West Lynn
Austin, Texas 78702

*People Buying Together
3335 Inwood
Dallas, Texas 75235

Community Association of
    Economic Development
2125 Littlepage Street
Fort Worth, Texas 76107

Southside Buyers Club
1600 Richmond Street
Fort Worth, Texas 76104

Divine Light Mission
3400 Montrose Boulevard   803
Houston, Texas 77006

UTAH

Peoples Co-op
554 North 3rd Street
Salt Lake City, Utah 84116

Todahaidekani Nalyehe
    Bahooghan Beeahoota Inc.
P.O. Box 402
Bluff, Utah 84512

Halchiita Nalyehe Bahoogan
    Inc.
P.O. Box 45
Mexican Hat, Utah 84531

VERMONT

*Northeast Kingdom
    Cooperative
P.O. Box 272
Barton, Vermont 05822

Addison County Buyers Club
15 Main Street
Bristol, Vermont 05443

*New England Peoples Co-op
North Co-op
160 North Winoodki Avenue
Burlington, Vermont 05401

Onion River Food Co-op
77 Archibald Street
Burlington, Vermont 05401

Franklyn Co-op
Rural Delivery 4
Enosburg Falls, Vermont 05450

P.O. Box A46
Johnson State College
Johnson, Vermont 05656

A-L. Dorm
Goddard College
Plainfield, Vermont 05667

*New England Peoples Co-op
Central Co-op/The Grange
P.O. Box 59
Plainfield, Vermont 05667

Plainfield Co-op
P.O. Box 157
Plainfield, Vermont 05567

Pinch of Love
RFD 1
Putney, Vermont 05346

Putney Consumers' Co-op
P.O. Box 55
Putney, Vermont 05346

Independent Buyers Club
  Foundation
14 Evelyn Street
Rutland, Vermont 05701

Westburke Collective
P.O. Box 62
West Burke, Vermont 05871

*Northeast Kingdon Co-op
P.O. Box 63A
West Clover, Vermont 05875

VIRGINIA

Pittsylvanis County Community
  Buying Club
P.O. Box 936
Chatham, Virginia 24531

Twin Oaks
Louisa, Virginia 23093

Charrlettsville Food Co-op
Route 1, P.O. Box 45A
Roseland, Virginia 22967

WASHINGTON

Community Food Co-op
1100 Harris Street
Bellingham, Washington 98225

Low-Income Meat & Produce
  Co-op
2512 Eldridge Avenue
Bellingham, Washington 98225

Clovergreen Co-op
23017 45th Avenue SE
Bethell, Washington 98011

Fertile Earth Foods
17226 Sunset Road
Bothell, Washington 98011

Chelan-Manson Natural Food
P.O. Box 153
Chelan, Washington 98816

Skagit Valley Food Co-op
619 2nd Street
Mount Vernon, Washington
  98273

Olympia Food Coop
904 East 4th
Olympia, Washington 98502

The Food Co-op
617 Tyler Street, P.O. Box 778
Port Townsend, Washington
  98368

Pullman Food Co-op
Northeast 850 A Street
Pullman, Washington 99163

Roslyn Common Market
P.O. Box 356
Roslyn, Washington 98941

Capitol Hill Co-op
1835 12th Avenue
Seattle, Washington 98122

*Co-op Community Grains
4030 22 Avenue W.
Seattle, Washington 98199

*Cooperating Community
  Natural Foods
Seattle Community Produce
1510 Pike Place
Seattle, Washington 98101

Corner Produce
90 Pike Street
Seattle, Washington 98101

Little Bread
8050 Lake City Way, N.E.
Seattle, Washington 98115

Peace, Bread & Love Band
P.O. Box 12664
Seattle, Washington 98111

*Puget Consumers Co-op
2165 65th Avenue, N.E.
Seattle, Washington 98115

The Store
1919 West 2nd
Spokane, Washington 99204

Food Bag
914 Broadway
Tacoma, Washington 98402

WEST VIRGINIA

Freeman, Wolf, & Associated
  Communities Buying Club
Freeman, West Virginia 24724

WISCONSIN

Boscobel Marketing Co-op
Route 4
Boscobel, Wisconsin 53805

Connorsville Co-op
Route 2, P.O. Box 110
Boyceville, Wisconsin 54725

Westside Food Store
602 Water Street
Eau Claire, Wisconsin 54701

Menominee County Co-op
Keshena, Wisconsin 54135

*Common Market, Limited
1340 East Washington
Madison, Wisconsin 53703

Eagle Heights Co-op
611 Eagle Heights
Madison, Wisconsin 53704

East Side Grocery Co-op
2406 Hoard
Madison, Wisconsin 53703

Intergalactic Co-op
119 West Gorham
Madison, Wisconsin 53703

*Intra-Community Cooperative
1335 Gilson Street
Madison, Wisconsin 53715

*Madison Community Co-op
(Information Center for Madison
   co-ops)
1001 University Avenue
Madison, Wisconsin 53715

Miflin Street Co-op
32 North Bassett
Madison, Wisconsin 53703

W.S.A. Store
720 State
Madison, Wisconsin 53103

*Whole Earth Learning
   Community
817 East Johnson Street
Madison, Wisconsin 53703

Menominee Buying Club
1814 East 17th Avenue
Menominee, Wisconsin 54751

Fertile Dirt Co-op
Restaurant and Bakery
316 West Juneau
Milwaukee, Wisconsin 53203

Milwaukee Food Buying Co-op
1234 South 16th Street
Milwaukee, Wisconsin 53204

Outpost Natural Foods Co-op
833 East Locust
Milwaukee, Wisconsin 53212

People's Food Co-op, Limited
814 East Clarke
Milwaukee, Wisconsin 53212

Good Life Natural Foods
600 North Main
Oshkosh, Wisconsin 54901

Head Start Food Co-op
1315 North Wisconsin Avenue
Racine, Wisconsin 53402

Rice Sake Co-op
1103 West Knapp Street
Rice Lake, Wisconsin 54868

Whole Earth
Route 3
River Falls, Wisconsin 54022

Stevens Point Area Food Co-op
2501 Welsby Avenue
Stevens Point, Wisconsin 54481

Superior Food Buying Club
904 Tower Avenue
Superior, Wisconsin 54880

WYOMING

Mother Jenkins
28th Street and O'Neil
Cheyenne, Wyoming 82001

Whole Earth Grainery
Laramie Peoples Market
111 Ivinson Street
Laramie, Wyoming 82070

CANADA

*Hub Co-op
250 Albert Street
Nanaimo, British Columbia

Cooperative D'Ailments
Naturales et Macrobiotiques
4616 Panieau
Montreal, Quebec

Karma Food Co-op
Dupont Street
Toronto, Ontario

Natures Way
Etherea Natural Food
341 Bloor
Toronto, Ontario

Banyan Tree
474 Jesse Street
Winnepeg, Manitoba

Wholesale Food Suppliers

This list has been compiled from information solicited from individual food co-ops throughout the country. The comments under the suppliers' names are from various food co-ops. Particular care and knowledge is necessary in the purchase of meat, and the individual sources have not been checked by the author. (See Chapter 11 on meat buying.)

It is impossible to know whether a product is truly "organic" or "natural" solely from this list. It is the responsibility of the individual co-op to determine the reputability of a particular supplier. Check out local sources. Shipping charges can be prohibitive from distant suppliers. Make comparisons.

The federations listed in chapter are also good sources for wholesale supplies.

ARKANSAS

**Shiloh Farms
P.O. Box 97
Highway 59
Sulphur Springs, Arkansas
  72768

Shiloh operates a natural foods bakery and wholesale food delivery service in all but about five states in the Pacific Northwest. All grains and flours are kept under refrigeration instead of being fumigated. Dairy products, grains, and cereals, baked goods, meat, dried fruits, juices, fresh fruits (in season only)

CALIFORNIA

Viebrock Farms
1570 Cox Road
Aptos, California 95033

(**) National distributor
(*) Ships out of state but usually within a specific radius

Ecology Trading Center
788 Old County Road
Belmont, California 94002

The Body Shop
2566 Telegraph Avenue
Berkeley, California 94704

Challenge Cream & Butter
708 Addison Street
Berkeley, California 94710

Earth Mother Flowers
1731 Ward Street
Berkeley, California 94703

One World Family
2340 Piedmond Avenue
Berkeley, California 94707
Organic

Real Good Bread
1700 Marin Avenue
Berkeley, California 94707

Vitality Co.
1122 Spruce Street
Berkeley, California 94707

Westbrae Natural Foods
1336 Gilman Street
Berkeley, California 94706
Wholesale distributors

Camp Joy
Boulder Creek, California 95006
Farmers of organic produce and
    flowers

All American Nut Co.
16901 Valley View Avenue
Cerritos, California 90701
Wholesalers of all kinds of nuts
    and nut butters

*Chico San
1262 Humboldt Avenue
Chico, California 95926
Grain

**Covalda Date Co.
P.O. Box 908
51-392 Highway 86
Coachella, California 94124
Dates, pecans naturally grown
    for 30 years; rather expensive
    but very good; they
    defumigate their dates

Millers Honey Co.
Laurel Street at Miller Drive
Colton, California 92324

Kahan & Lessin Co.
3131 East Maria Street
Compton, California 90222

*Erewhon Trading Co.
8454 Steller Drive
Culver City, California 90230
Grain

Golden Farms
Route 1, Box 1160-B
Durham, California 95938

Acme Juicerator Co.
Route 1, P.O. Box 1550 B
Elk Grove, California 95624

National Biscuit Co.
4240 Hollis
Emeryville, California 94608

Joe Hamada
875 Eolus
Encinitas California 92024
  (home)
Farm 1/4 mile south of Palomar
  Road on El Camino in
  Carlsbad

Phil Arena
2109 Miller
Escondido, California 92025
"Probably the best organic
  farmer in Southern
  California"

Bill Stretton
3974 Reche Road
Fallbrook, California 92028
Citrus, avocados, good grower

Marbo Quality Foods, Inc.
P.O. Box 3111
Fresno, California 93766

Peoples Union Co-op Farm
8734 West Manning Avenue
Fresno, California 93706

Hathaway Allied Products
24002 Frampton Avenue
Harbor City, California 90710

Fresh Pak Products, Inc.
P.O. Box 74
Hayward, California 94543

Hemet Egg Ranch
25356 North Hemet Street
Hemet, California 92343
Paul & Valma Verbanick
  really fertile, natural eggs
  and chickens

Ocean View Mushroom Farms
Huntington Beach
18196 Golden West
Huntington Beach, California
  92646
Very large producer

Ecology Club
2137 Laguna Canyon Road
Laguna Beach, California 92651

Penny Dorado makes hand
  lotion, face cream, aftershave,
  etcetera from pure Erewhon
  oils, beeswax, good stuff

Central Market
4th and Hill Street
Los Angeles, California
Produce

*Mushrooms, Inc.
510 East Olympic Boulevard
Los Angeles, California 90015
Produce

Northern Produce Co.
1000 South Wall Street
Los Angeles, California 90015

**Organic Foods and Gardens
2655 Commerce Way
Los Angeles, California 90022
Distributors and wholesalers of
    organic foods

Smart and Final
2115 Pico Boulevard
Los Angeles, California
Canned goods and packaged
    goods (#10 cans and larger
    sizes)

Warner Foods
2522 East 37th Street
Los Angeles, California 90058
Meats and seafood

Faia Sales Co.
2888 El Presidio
Long Beach, California 90810

Ranch Market
1193 Fremont Avenue
Monterey, California 93940
Distributors, brown fertile eggs
    (Andersons), organic produce

Andersons Egg House
Watsonville Road
Morgan Hill, California 95037

Buzzard Bay Co.
324 63rd Street
Oakland, California 94618

Cal Ben Co.
9828 Pearmain Street
Oakland, California 94603

The Food Mill
3033 MacArthur Boulevard
Oakland, California 94602

E. F. Lane & Son
744 Kevin Court
Oakland, California 94621

Peerless Coffee Co., Inc.
926 Washington Street
Oakland, California 94607

*Rainbow Pure Foods
6616 Woodland Place
Oakland, California 94611

Ranch Pak Eggs
401 Jackson Street
Oakland, California 94607

Shabazz Bakery
8740 East 14th Street
Oakland, California 94607
Natural foods (Black Muslim),
    bakery, breads and pastries

Specialty Bakers
1940 East 14th Street
Oakland, California 94606

Tuttle Cheese Co.
2401 Union Street
Oakland, California 94607

West Coast Produce Co.
317 Franklin Street
Oakland, California 94607

Your Bakery
806 Calmar
Oakland, California 94610

Braber Olives
P.O. Box 511
Ontario, California 91764

Whole Earth Bakery
405 University Avenue
Palo Alto, California 94301
Real good leavened and
    unleavened natural foods,
    bread, also pastries

Fred Adams
18516 Rural Delivery 248
Porterville, California 93257
Farmer distributor, natural olives

Graham Ck. Ranch
Route 5, P.O. Box 151
Porterville, California 93257

*Associated Co-operatives, Inc.
4801 Central Avenue
Richmond, California 94804
Groceries, fresh fruits and
    vegetables, fresh meats.
    Distribute in California only in
    a 100-mile radius from
    Richmond

Wm. Smeds & Sons
6469 South Holbrook Avenue
Reedley, California 93654

Daisy Fresh Yogurt Co.
P.O. Box 4295-JA
Riverside, California 92504
Natural culture for your own
    yogurt

Asvattha—Tree of Life
P.O. Box 69
San Anselmo, California 94960

Everybody's Distribution Co.
1201 San Anselmo Avenue
San Anselmo, California 94960
New age raw juices

Don-Glo Ranch
551 Cardiff Avenue
San Bernardino, California
    92408
Naturally raised beef

Jim Small
25 West Islay
Santa Barbara, California 93101
Distributes Mexican fruit from
Tijuana market

Sunburst Organic Foods
4444 Hollister Avenue
Santa Barbara, California 93105
Farmers and distributors of
organic fruits and produce

Central Coast Organic Grower's
Co-op
1920 Maciel Avenue
Santa Cruz, California 95060
Distributors of local organic
produce

Granola Shop
550 Palm
Santa Cruz, California 95060
Good granola in bulk, also
packaged

Harmony Foods
232 Amat Street
Santa Cruz, California 95060
Distributors and
wholesalers—bulk natural
foods and candy

Karmananda
1195 Thompson
Santa Cruz, California 95060

Primaterra
2115 Ocean Street
Santa Cruz, California 90005

Staff of Life Bakery
1305 Water Street
Santa Cruz, California 95060
Natural foods, bakery breads,
and pastries

California Vulcan Macaroni Co.
5990 3rd Street
San Francisco, California 94124

Capricorn Coffees, Inc.
1555 Fillmore Street
San Francisco, California 94115

Coast-Dakota Flour
1588 Carroll Avenue
San Francisco, California 94124

Excelsior Incense Works
P.O. Box 31233
San Francisco, California 94131

Guistos
241 East Horns Avenue
San Francisco, California
Bakery and natural foods (lots of
grains, beans, sea salt, seeds)

*Herb T
P.O. Box 6377
San Francisco, California 94101

Hirschfelder Co.
1051 Howard Street
San Francisco, California 94103

Landstrom
P.O. Box 2886
336 Oyster Point Boulevard
South San Francisco, California
Wholesaler, health food
  merchandiser. Big company,
  all sorts of stuff

Monarch Flour Co.
465 California Street
San Francisco, California 94084

M.C.B.
P.O. Box 24262
San Francisco, California 94124

Organic Merchants
1384 9th Avenue
San Francisco, California 92082

Nippon Co.
1426 Minnesota Street
San Francisco, California 94107
Wholesale distributors, cheap,
  not organic brown rice

Scandia Finer Foods Co.
130 Potrero Avenue
San Francisco, California 94103

Spiral Foods, Inc.
56 Ringold Street
San Francisco, California 94103
Miso, tamari, etcetera

Sunshine Biscuits, Inc.
P.O. Box 37442
San Francisco, California 94137

Sun Valley Dairy Co.
300 Alemany Boulevard West
San Francisco, California 94110

Monterey Cheese Co.
P.O. Box 2487
South San Francisco, California
  94084

Oroweat Baking Co.
264 South Spruce Avenue
South San Francisco, California
  94080

Bernard Food Industries
P.O. Box 487
San Jose, California 95103

Garden City Pottery Co.
560 North Sixth Street
San Jose, California 95106

New Age Distribution Co., Inc.
795 West Hedding Street
San Jose, California 95126

Pottery Sales
1341 Martin Avenue
San Jose, California 95126

*Pure and Simple
795 West Hedding Street
San Jose, California 95126

Vitality Farms Co.
P.O. Box 8441
San Jose, California 95125

*The Well
795 West Hedding Street
San Jose, California 95126
Grain, flours, butters, dried
   fruit, eggs, produce

Zoria Farms & Co.
234 North Capital Avenue
San Jose, California 95127
Organic produce, dried fruit,
   farmers and distributors

Stella D'Oro Biscuit Co.
1000 Montague
San Leandro, California 94577

Middle East Bakery
1529 South B Street
San Mateo, California 94401

The Master Baker
861 Del Ganado Road
San Rafael, California 94903

Natural Food Commissary
P.O. Box 1051
San Rafael, California 94902

West Coast Organic Food
941 Bloomfield Road
Sebastopol, California 95472

Gregory Walls
3121 North Main Street
Soquel, California 95073
Honey in 55-gallon drums,
   60-lb. tins

New Morning Bakery
237 South Murphy Avenue
Sunnyvale, California 94086

Yorgos Savides
224 Buck Avenue
Vacaville, California 95688

*Jaffe Brothers
28560 Lilack Road
Valley Center, California 92082
Conservative old-line organic
   people. Now have a cheap
   medium-grain brown rice

F.C. Thomas
1435 Alta Vista
Vista, California 92083
Fine honey

Vita-Green Farms
P.O. Box 878
Vista, California 92083
Middleman for expensive
   organic stuff

Age of Foods, Inc.
P.O. Box 1511
West Arcadia, California 91006

Wm. T. Thompson Co.
23529 South Figueroa Street
Wilmington, California 90744

Prairie Gold Bakery
13378 California Street
Yucaipa, California 92399
Gets his own grains, mills them,
    makes good bread, although
    not for everyone's taste

COLORADO

Butternut Bakery
30th Street and Valmont Street
Boulder, Colorado
Day-old bread

Celestial Seasonings
P.O. Box 1405
Boulder, Colorado 80302

Green Mountain Grains
Arapahoe
Boulder, Colorado
Grains and beans

King Soupers
Crossroads Shopping Center
Boulder, Colorado
Sides of beef

Watts Hardy
2790 Walnut
Boulder, Colorado 80302
Cheese wholesalers

Associated Grocers
51st and Broadway
Denver, Colorado
Grains

Denver Tomato
207 Demargo Market
Denver, Colorado 80216
Produce wholesalers

Pennington
5585 East 47th Avenue
Denver, Colorado 80216
Wholesalers of canned and
    frozen foods

Rocky Mountain Fruit and
    Produce
Denargo Market
29th and Broadway
Denver, Colorado

Colorado Organic Growers
    Market Association
c/o Judd & Terry Blaine
Ft. Lupton, Colorado 80621

**Cliffrose
129 Coffman
Longmont, Colorado 80501
Grain wholesalers

CONNECTICUT

*Pilch Organic Gardens, Inc.
Moody Road
P.O. Box P
Hazardville Station
Enfield, Connecticut 05082

GEORGIA

Federation of Southern Co-ops
20 Marietta Street, N.W.
Room 1200
52 Fairlie Street, N.W.
Atlanta, Georgia 30303

Eastern Georgia Farmers' Co-op
P.O. Box 35
Waynesboro, Georgia 30830
Mr. Clark Edmonds, manager.
   Financed and organized by the
   Rural Advancement Fund of
   the National Sharecroppers
   Fund, Inc. Ships to eastern
   U.S. area. Organic Products

ILLINOIS

Arthur Cheeses Co.
320 East Second Street
Arthur, Illinois 61911
Danish swiss

Anton-Argires Bros.
13 South Water Market
Chicago, Illinois 60608

Banner
111-115 South Water Market
Chicago, Illinois 60608

Albert Barnett
56-58 South Water Market
Chicago, Illinois 60608

Battaglia
15 South Water Market
Chicago, Illinois 60608

Capodice-Gringic
47 South Water Market
Chicago, Illinois 60608

Caravetta Foods
1246 West Randolph
Chicago, Illinois 60607
Parmesan cheese

Caruso Produce
12 South Water Market
Chicago, Illinois 60608

George Cornille and Sons
60 South Water Market
Chicago, Illinois 60608

L. Frankel
224 North Peoria
Chicago, Illinois 60608
Beef, veal, pork, corned beef

*Georgia Nuts
3325 North California Avenue
Chicago, Illinois 60618
Distributor

Glenn and Anderson
825-35 West Wayman
Chicago, Illinois 60607
Bacon, hams, pork loins, pig's
  feet, sausage, wieners

Gridley, Maxon and Co.
27-31 South Water Market
Chicago, Illinois 60608

H and S Provisions
1135-37 West Lake Street
Chicago Fulton Street Market
Chicago, Illinois 60607
Hams, salami, beef roasts

La Mantia Bros.
28-32 South Water Market
Chicago, Illinois 60608

Mahoney, Cunningham,
  and De Vic
1156 West Randolph
Chicago, Illinois 60607
Blue cheese, American cheese,
  margarine

Merkel
23-25 South Water Market
Chicago, Illinois 60608

Neiman Bros.
3322 West Newport
Chicago, Illinois 60618
Flour

Louis Snyder and Sons
169 South Water Market
Chicago, Illinois 60608
Chickens and other poultry

Town and Country
98 South Water Market
Chicago, Illinois 60608

Vitamins, Inc.
401 North Michigan Avenue
Chicago, Illinois 60611

Vitro and Pecoraro Co.
46 South Water Market
Chicago, Illinois 60608

Wainer Fruit
19 South Water Market
Chicago, Illinois 60608

Food for Life
420 Wrightwood
Elmhurst, Illinois 60126

Pembroke Farmers Co-op
P.O. Box 62
Hopkins Park, Illinois 60954

Home Juice Company
15th and Bloomingdale
Melrose Park, Illinois 60160

Co-operative Food Distributors
of America
505 Park Place
Park Ridge, Illinois 60068
Trade association for retailer
owned—lists of suppliers

Homestead Community Bakery
St. Joseph, Illinois 61873

KANSAS

Linn Country Food Growers
Association
P.O. Box 447
Pleasantown, Kansas 66075

KENTUCKY

Grindmaster of Kentucky
745 West Main Street
Louisville, Kentucky 40202
Rent a peanut-butter grinder,
also cashew-butter grinder

MAINE

*Kennebunk Chemical Center
Railroad Avenue
Kennebunk, Maine 04043

MARYLAND

Wm. G. Scarlett and Co.
608 President Street
Baltimore, Maryland 21202

**Laurelbrook Natural Foods
P.O. Box 47
Bel Air, Maryland 21014
A distributor of Deaf Smith,
Chico San, Erewhon and other
"first foods"

Devcor
Route 1
P.O. Box 129
Freeland, Maryland 21053
Farmer-consumer co-op, apples,
peaches, oranges, eggs, and
some vegetables

Glut
4005 34th Street
Mt. Rainer, Maryland 20812
A central buying and storage
house for Greater
Washington's many co-op
food centers and smaller
neighborhood buying clubs

*Potomac Cooperatives, Inc.
8547 Piney Branch Road
Silver Springs, Maryland 20901
(Warehouse member of
   Cooperative League of
   U.S.A. Food plus other items)

MASSACHUSETTS

Maple Farm
Old Hardwick Road
Barre, Massachusetts 01005
Organic poultry and vegetable

**Erewhon, Inc.
33 Farnsworth Street
Boston, Massachusetts 02210
One of the largest suppliers of
   natural food stores and co-ops:
   grains, cereals, flours, beans,
   seeds and nuts, tamari and
   miso, tea, sea vegetables,
   dried fruit, juice and vinegar,
   vegetable oil, butters, honey,
   condiments, soaps, knives,
   rice, bags, pressure cookers

Natural Recipes
44 Robinwood Avenue
Boston, Massachusetts 02130

**New England Federation of
   Co-ops
*The Boston Co-op
Babbit Street
Boston, Massachusetts 02215
Complete supplies

Attar
31 Putnam Avenue
Cambridge, Massachusetts
   02139

Sands Taylor & Wood Co.
130 Fawcett Street
Cambridge, Massachusetts
   02138

Archibald and Kendall
255 Maverick Street
East Boston, Massachusetts
   02128

*New England Co-operatives,
   Inc.
160 Fountain Street
Framingham, Massachusetts
   01702
Dry goods for Eastern and
   Central New England

*Infinity Products are distributed
   in New England by
Llama, Toucan & Crow, Inc.
60 Bank Row
Greenfield, Massachusetts
   01301

*Preston Fuel Co.
Lowell, Massachusetts

Columbo and Sons
Methuen, Massachusetts 01844
Yogurt

Specialty Products of New
England
North Attleboro, Massachusetts
02703

On The Rise Natural Bakery
Orange, Massachusetts 01364

All Star Dairy Foods, Inc.
Columbo Yogurt
456 Newton Street
South Hadley, Massachusetts
01075

MICHIGAN

Ann Arbor People's Produce Co.
2955 Hilltop
Ann Arbor, Michigan 48103

*Eden Foods, Inc.
330 Maynard Street
Ann Arbor, Michigan 48108
Complete line of grains, flour,
pasta, nuts, oil, butter, juice,
snacks, cereals. Range of
distribution is mainly all of
Michigan and Ohio and
Eastern Indiana—a 200-250
mile radius of extension from
Ann Arbor

Kinagro Farms
Rural Route 1
Belding, Michigan 48809
Apples and cider

Boone's Farm
Route 4, P.O. Box 181-3
Big Rapids, Michigan 49307

Full Circle Farm
466 Farrand Road, Route 3
Bronson, Michigan 49028

Dean Granzow Organic Gardens
8520 Dixie Highway
Clarkston, Michigan 48016

Tom Fanos Association
18621 West Seven Mile Road
Detroit, Michigan 48219

Richard Osterbeck
Route 1, Hinman Road
Eagle, Michigan 48822
Grain

Family of Man
541 East Grand River
East Lansing, Michigan 48823

Wolf Moon Bakery
233 Beal Street
East Lansing, Michigan 48823
Bread and granola

Dale Kunkel
7427 Island Highway
Eaton Rapids, Michigan 48827
Carrots and onions

Associated Wild Rice
1415 Highway 169 East
Grand Rapids, Michigan 55744

Ferry Farmers
Route 1
Hesperia, Michigan 49421

Don Malkin
Rural Route 2, P.O. Box 35B
Laingsburg, Michigan 48848
Vegetables

Wolf Moon Bakery
714 South Hayford
Lansing, Michigan 48912
Co-op bakery

Organic Growers of Michigan
Paul Shultz
Route 1, P.O. Box 26
Lawrence, Michigan 49064

Sunshower Co-op Farm
Route 1, P.O. Box 26
Lawrence, Michigan 49064

Happy Farmer Co-op
c/o Jean Demski
Route 3
Shelby, Michigan 49455

MINNESOTA

Bailey Farm Community
Rural Route 1, P.O. Box 112
Altura, Minnesota 55910

*Midland Co-operatives, Inc.
(Consumer Goods Division,
Food/Clothing Department)
217 Lake Avenue
Duluth, Minnesota 55803
Will deliver approximately 150
miles from Duluth if on a
delivery route

Meadow Farm
Route 1
Erhard, Minnesota 56534

Grainhead Productions
P.O. Box 14213
University Station
Minneapolis, Minnesota 55414

Organic Growers and Buyers
c/o E.L.M.
1222 Southeast 4th Street
Minneapolis, Minnesota 55414

East Central Farmers, Inc.
Rutledge, Minnesota 55778

MISSOURI

Great Plains Distribution Co.
240 Oak Street
Kansas City, Missouri 64106

MONTANA

*Ravalli County Dairy
P.O. Box 207
Ravalli, Montana 59863

NEW HAMPSHIRE

New England Wholesale Market
Chelsea, New Hampshire
Produce

**Attar
Smith Village
New Ipswich, New Hampshire
   03071
Will ship to any state as well as
   Canada; requirement: $25
   order

*Yellow House Bakery, Inc.
South Acworth, New Hampshire
   03607

South Co-op, Natural Organic
   Farmers Association
52 Main Street
West Lebanon, New Hampshire
   03746
Organic foods

NEW JERSEY

**Mideastern Co-op, Inc.
75 Amor Avenue
Carlstadt, New Jersey 07072
Dry goods, Mid-Atlantic states
   only

**Rocky Hollow Herb Farm,
   Inc.
P.O. Box 215
Lake Wallkill Road
Sussex, New Jersey 07461

NEW MEXICO

Cliffrose-Dist.
Las Vegas, New Mexico 87701
Grain

NEW YORK

Shadowfax
25 North Depot Street
Binghamton, New York 13901

Elma Foods
4856 Lake Avenue
Blasdell, New York 14219
Organic

Buffalo Nut Shop
2964 Main Street
Buffalo, New York 14214

Federal Baker's Supply Corp.
300 Scajaquada Street
Buffalo, New York 14211

McCullagh Coffee
2208 Elmwood Avenue
Buffalo, New York 14223
Coffee, tea

Sorrento Cheese Co.
2375 South Park Avenue
Buffalo, New York 14220

Buttercup Farms
Central Square, New York
    13036
Cheese

Clarks Natural Herbs
Chafee, New York 14030
Organic

*Kutter's Cheese Factory
Route 5
Corfu, New York 14036
Has been given a good word

Minnamere Farm
472 East Shore Road
Great Neck, New York 11024
Jersey raw milk

Deer Valley Farms
Guilford, New York 13780
Retail and wholesale beef, eggs,
    chickens, produce, grains,
    sells other farmers organic
    produce and lamb

Stur-Dee Health Products
Austin Boulevard
Island Park, New York 11558

Somadhara Bakery
DeWitt Mall
Ithaca, New York 14850
Bread

Dannon
22-11 38th Avenue
Long Island City, New York
    11101

The Food Warehouse
35-10 Northern Boulevard
Long Island City, New York
    11101

*Japan Foods
P.O. Box 6090
Long Island City, New York
    11106

NEW YORK CITY

Bronx Terminal Market
151st Street at Exterior Street
Bronx, New York 10451
Eggs, produce, cheese, butter,
　　bacon, flowers

Hunts Point Market
East Bay Avenue
Hunts Point
Bronx, New York 10474
Eggs, produce, cheese, butter,
　　bacon, flowers

Velvel Kosher Meat Corp.
41-85 Main Street
Flushing, New York 11355

Glen Alden
10 Jones Street
New York, New York 10014
Butter

*Aphrodesia
28 Carmine Street
New York, New York 10014
Herbs and spices

Basior-Schwartz
421 West 14th Street
New York, New York 10014
Meat

**A. I. Brazzini Co.
339 Greenwich Street
New York, New York 10013
Nuts and dried fruits, all U.S.

Buchsbaum
608 West 40th Street
New York, New York 10018
Meat

Glenmere
367 Greenwich Street
New York, New York 10013
Eggs, bacon

Hillside Butter & Egg
11 Jay Street
New York, New York 10013
Eggs, butter, cheese

*Infinity Co., Inc.
173 Duane Street
New York, New York 10013
All products are natural foods,
　　free of all additives, unless
　　stated organic. Whole grains,
　　rice, beans, seeds, fruits, and
　　nuts

**Kiebl's Pharmacy
109 3rd Avenue
New York, New York 10003
Herbs, essential oils, cosmetics,
　　shampoos, etcetera

MAR Wholesale Meats
672 Hudson Street
New York, New York 10014

*Mottel Health Foods, Inc.
451 Washington Street
New York, New York 10013
Peanuts, beans, spices serves the
    East coast and parts of the
    Midwest and Texas (has been
    given a good word), all natural
    bulk grains

Old Bohemian
452 West 13th Street
New York, New York 10014
Meat

T.A. White
444 West 14th Street
New York, New York 10014
Bacon

*Joseph A. Zaloom Co. Inc.
8 Jay Street
New York, New York 10013
300-lb. bulk, nuts, figs, seeds,
    dried fruits, soybeans, no
    guarantee as to natural

Shadowfax
Rural Delivery 5
Pleasant Hill Road
Port Crane, New York 13833
Wholesaler in natural and
    organic foods in bulk and
    packaged

Blessed Thistle Bakery
942 Monroe Street
Rochester, New York 14620
Wholesale breads, cookies, and
    granola

Clear Eye
713 Monroe Avenue
Rochester, New York 14607
Warehouse supplying food
    co-ops in western New York,
    Rochester, Buffalo, and
    Syracuse

Craft People's Co-op
72 East Avenue
Rochester, New York 14604

**Niblack Foods, Inc.
20 Magnolia Street
Rochester, New York 14608
Products normally distributed by
    regional specialty jobbers
    throughout the U.S. and
    Canada, grains, cereals, flour

Hood Co.
80 West Circular Street
Saratoga, New York 12866
Yogurt and cottage cheese

*Goodman International
30 South Main Street
Spring Valley, New York 10977
Cosmetics (natural)

Koskiney Farms
Trumansburg, New York 14886
Eggs

Barth Nutritional Supplement
270 West Merrick Road
Valley Stream, New York 11582

Blessed Thistle Bakery (Co-op)
510 Lake Road
Webster, New York 14580

*Return Co.
P.O. Box 373
Woodstock, New York 12498

NORTH CAROLINA

Harmony
West Franklin Street
Chapel Hill, North Carolina
  27514
Retailer, will wholesale, gives
  discount for bulk grains

William T. Hatfield
Macon County, North Carolina
  27551
Organic cider (pasteurized)

Southwestern North Carolina
  Farmers Co-op
P.O. Box 674
Murphy, North Carolina 28906

Coastal Growers Association
P.O. Box 490
Rose Hill, North Carolina 28458

Carolina Soap & Candle
Southern Pines, North Carolina
  28387

NORTH DAKOTA

Pioneer Specialty Foods
P.O. Box 427
Fargo, North Dakota 58102

OHIO

Worthington Foods, Inc.
900 Proprietors Road
Worthington, Ohio 43085

OREGON

*Nichols Garden Nursery
1190 North Pacific Highway
Albany, Oregon 97321
Hops with recipes, sour
  doughs—hopbread,
  winemaking

Rogue Valley Creamery
211 North Pacific Highway
Central Point, Oregon 97501
Milk products

Starflower
1936-1/2 Willamette
Eugene, Oregon 97405
Nuts, fruits, teas, organic foods,
    excellent for rennetless cheese

Rogue Gold Dairy, Inc.
P.O. Box 379
Grants Pass, Oregon 97526

Big Foot Beef Distributors
175 East California Street
Jacksonville, Oregon 97530

Northwest Grocery
Medford, Oregon 97501

Sunray Orchards
Myrtle Creek, Oregon 97457

*East Earth Herb
Route 3, P.O. Box 181
Reedsport, Oregon 97467

Springfield Creamery
145 North 3rd Street
Springfield, Oregon 97477
Yogurt

PENNSYLVANIA

**Nature's Products
2020 Hamilton Street
Allentown, Pennsylvania 18104

Village Market
Boyertown, Pennsylvania 19512
Pure goat products

*Worldwide Produce
Boyertown, Pennsylvania 19512
Natural/organic produce shipped
    to 13 states

*Snowhill Farm
Rural Delivery 3
Coatesville, Pennsylvania 19320
Organic beef and veal

Better Foods Foundation, Inc.
33 North Washington Street
Greencastle, Pennsylvania
    17225

Mervin McMichael
Route 6, P.O. Box 63
Lancaster, Pennsylvania 15903
Natural eggs

*St. John's Dairy
New London, Pennsylvania
    19360
Raw milk

*Richard Higley Co.
Parkersburg, Pennsylvania
    19365
Natural cheese

Penn Argyl Milling Co.
Penn Argyl, Pennsylvania 18072

**Walnut Acres
Penns Creek, Pennsylvania
  17862
One of the oldest, best-known
  organic farms, grains stored,
  refrigerated without any
  preservatives or fumigants,
  etcetera, cereals, produce,
  meat, dairy, baked goods,
  salad dressings, etcetera, most
  items strictly organically
  raised; if not it is indicated on
  the label

Powelton Baking Co-op
3507 Race Street
Philadelphia, Pennsylvania
  19104
Natural bread, granola

RHODE ISLAND

*Bond Foods
10 Crary Street
Providence, Rhode Island 02903

Cavanaugh Co.
305 Putnam Avenue
Smithfield, Rhode Island

*Meadowbrook Herb Garden
Richmond Town House Road
Wyoming, Rhode Island 02898
Herbs and spices

TENNESSEE

Collegedale Distributors
Collegedale, Tennessee 37315

TEXAS

Manor Bakeries
Arlington, Texas 76010
Regular bread

City Farmer's Market
Dallas, Texas
Produce

*Arrowhead Mills
P.O. Box 866
Hereford, Texas 79045
Grains, rice, seeds, beans

Malcolm Beck
7561 East Evans Road
San Antonio, Texas 78209
Produce

VERMONT

*The Good Life
80 Main Street
Brattleboro, Vermont 05301
The most complete line of
  natural and organic foods in
  New England; herbs, spices,
  utensils, cheese, and wine.
  Everything available in bulk
  quantities at wholesale + 10%

*Lana, Touchan, Crow
Brattleboro, Vermont 05301

Chittenden Produce Co.
Burlington, Vermont 05401
Wholesaler

Cabot Creamery
Cabot, Vermont 05647

*Appleyard Corp.
Maple Corner
Calais, Vermont 05648

Frog Run Farm (Co-op)
East Charleston, Vermont 05833

Crowley Cheese
Healdville, Vermont 05147
Vermont cheddar mild, medium,
    or sharp, 3-lb. wheel 6.50,
    5-lb. wheel 9.00

Champlain Valley Apiaries
P.O. Box 127
Middlebury, Vermont 05753

*Pinch of Love Bakery
RFD 1
Putney, Vermont 05346

*Willis Wood
RFD 2, P.O. Box 266
Springfield, Vermont 05156

Maple Grove
167 Portland Street
St. Johnsbury, Vermont 05819

VIRGINIA

Southwest Virginia Growers
    Co-op
Route 2
Nickelsville, Virginia 24271

*Halifax County
    Co-op—Southern
Agricultural Association of
    Virginia
P.O. Box 734
South Boston, Virginia 24592
Financed and organized through
    the National Sharecroppers
    Fund

WASHINGTON

City Produce
710 7th Avenue South
Seattle, Washington 98104

*Co-operating Community
    Produce
1510 Pike Place
Seattle, Washington 98101
Wholesale organic produce,
    supplier for Pacific Northwest

Silverbow Honey Co.
Snohomish, Washington 98290

American Biscuit Co.
P.O. Box 418
South Tacoma, Washington
    98409

Langans Organic Foods
Route 2, P.O. Box 163
Toppenish, Washington 98948

WISCONSIN

Nature's Bakery
1101 Williamson Street
Madison, Wisconsin 53703

UW Provisions
Beld Street
Madison, Wisconsin
Meat wholesaler

*Lee Engineering Co.
2023 West Wisconsin Avenue
Milwaukee, Wisconsin 53201
Grain mills—all sizes for stone
    grinding

Kyser Cheese
Mt. Horeh, Wisconsin 53572
Raw milk, undyed cheese

Quercus Alba Bakery
Oregon, Wisconsin 54303